Poems Between Women

BETWEEN MEN ~ BETWEEN WOMEN
Lesbian and Gay Studies

Lillian Faderman and Larry Gross, Editors

Poems Between Women

FOUR CENTURIES OF LOVE, ROMANTIC FRIENDSHIP,
AND DESIRE

Edited by Emma Donoghue

COLUMBIA UNIVERSITY PRESS   NEW YORK

Columbia University Press
Publishers Since 1893
New York   Chichester, West Sussex
Copyright © 1997 Emma Donoghue
All rights reserved
The permissions on pp. 195–199 constitute an
extension of this copyright page.

Library of Congress Cataloging-in-Publication Data
Poems between women : four centuries of love, romantic friendship, and
   desire / edited by Emma Donoghue.
      p.   cm. — (Between men ~ between women)
   Includes index.
   ISBN 978-0-231-10924-6 (cloth) ISBN 978-0-231-10925-3 (pbk.)
   1. Love poetry, English.   2. English poetry—Women authors.
3. American poetry—Women authors.   4. Lesbians' writings, American.
5. Lesbians' writings, English.   6. Love poetry—Women authors.
7. Female friendship—Poetry.   8. Erotic poetry, American.
9. Erotic poetry, English.   10. Love poetry, American.
11. Women—Poetry.   I. Donoghue, Emma, 1969–   .   II. Series.
PR1184.P62   1997
821.008'09287—dc21   96–49693
                                                             CIP

Casebound editions of Columbia University Press books are printed on
permanent and durable acid-free paper.
Printed in the United States of America

This book is for Chris,
with my whole heart

A Health Warning

The homosexual unconsciously finds a magnetic quality
in words, and derives gratification from utterances ...
Rhyming is a favourite method of communication among
most homosexuals, especially those who practise tribadism.

M. Chideckel
Female Sex Perversion (1935)

CONTENTS

ACKNOWLEDGEMENTS

I am indebted for biographical information to many of the books in the 'Further Reading' list that follows the Introduction, but particularly to the most useful and entertaining reference book I own, *The Feminist Companion to Literature in English*, edited by Virginia Blain, Patricia Clements and Isobel Grundy (1990).

I am grateful to the staff of Cambridge University Library, the British Library, the Robarts Library at the University of Toronto, the New York Public Library and particularly to the overworked but welcoming volunteers at the Lesbian Archive and Information Centre and the Glasgow Women's Library.

Thank you very much to Mary Nyquist, Simon Jones and Gillian Rodger for suggesting poems; to Debra Westgate, Deborah Ballard, Carole Nelson, Silke Gluess and Maria Walsh for bringing them to life by reading them aloud; to Chris Roulston for endless listening; very special thanks to Gráinne Ní Dhúill and Ali Smith for detailed feedback on early drafts; eternal gratitude to Paula Bennett for faxing me five unobtainable poems; to Anne Habiby and Hélène Roulston, for putting me up in New York and Toronto respectively; to my editors Kate Jones and Ann Miller; and, as ever, to my agent Caroline Davidson.

INTRODUCTION

Poems Between Women

'What Sappho would have said had her leap cured instead of killing her' is the name of a poem by Christina Rossetti. The phrase suggests a poet whose fragmentary texts continue to haunt her readers, who keeps coming back to get the last word in edgeways. But this anthology is not about the seventh-century BC poet of Lesbos and all she so inimitably said; instead, it gathers together poems of romantic friendship, love and desire by her spiritual descendants, the Sapphos of the last four centuries.

'Sappho' is not simply a euphemism for 'lesbian'; I am using the word here to include all those women poets who wrote about (among other things) passionate relations between women. It intrigues me that even poets who seem to have lived entirely heterosexual lives wrote the occasional poem in which love for women flares up. Poetry seems to have provided a space for such inconsistencies, a stage for those moments that complicate our views of sexuality and friendship. There are many excellent anthologies of contemporary self-defined lesbian poets on the market, but this is not one; it covers a broader spectrum, in an attempt to push beyond the identity politics of the 1980s and make thought-provoking connections across the boundary lines of sexual orientation and history.

What interest me more than the poets are the poems, those ambiguous, often playful texts which can present themselves as slices of life but are not so simple. Some are *about* love between women, others inspired *by* women, others written *to* particular women; when something about a poet's real-life relationships seems relevant to a particular poem, it will be found in the biographical notes at the back. But even the ones marked as autobiographical by a dedication or a title are all crafted, all in some sense fantasies; experience and emotion have been transformed in the writing.

My criteria for choosing these poems were simple. First, they were all written in English by women, and, as far as I have been able to ascertain, addressed to, aimed at or inspired by women. Second, they seem to me to be poems of love; they express, interrogate, are fuelled by or otherwise act out a variety of historical and contemporary forms of love between women. However, I have limited this vast field by not including poems to mothers, daughters or sisters, nor poems of plain friendship; I have sought to capture a certain quality of passion. My third and final criterion is that I like them.

My main aim has been variety of content and tone. The poets range from the famous and canonical to the totally unknown; I was delighted to resurrect so many startlingly good poems by writers long forgotten. As usual in a historical anthology, most of these poets are white and from the middle or upper classes, but some working-class women and women of colour can be found too. Again, the majority are from England or the United States, but I include quite a few who lived in Canada or Europe (mostly Ireland, Scotland, France and Italy), as well as a scattering from Australia and New Zealand, South America, India and Africa. Inevitably my selection is skewed towards the places where I was able to do extensive research.

But some of my omissions are more deliberate. I have left out many fascinating seventeenth- and eighteenth-century poems because they are too long and obscure in grammar and vocabulary to be easily enjoyed by modern readers. Also missing are poems of simple praise, classics widely available elsewhere and quite a few famous names. What most clearly distinguishes this collection from others is its emphasis on the historical range of poetry between women. Living poets (twenty out of my total of 106) are represented by one poem each; readers hungry for more should try the contemporary anthologies in the 'Further Reading' list.

All these poems have been published before. I have occasionally modernized spelling and removed italicization where it seemed likely to confuse or irritate. Rather than attempting to assign a single nationality to these often well-travelled women, I have listed their countries of residence after their names. The poems are arranged chronologically for easy access, and to show each poet in the context of her time and her peers. Since this is the first anthology to trace the long tradition of poems of passion between women, I have wanted to provide a clear map of how fashions have waxed and waned over four centuries.

Innocent Love? Seventeenth-century Beginnings

At the end of the twentieth century, when passionate love between women is seen by some as a minority lifestyle, by others as a stigma, by still others as a crime, it can be hard to remember that for most of the period covered by this anthology such attachment has been (in certain permitted forms) not just acceptable but highly valued in Western societies.

In the seventeenth century, upper- and middle-class women of leisure lived fairly separate lives from their men and were encouraged to devote much of their time and energy to loving – and celebrating in letters and poems – their female friends. Such love, usually designated since the 1970s by the eighteenth-century term 'romantic friendship', was generally assumed to be a serious emotional partnership, sincere, unselfish, loyal, physically affectionate but not sexual, and conducive to piety, good works, other friendships and marriage.

But awareness of woman-to-woman sexual practices circulated in a subterranean way. Working-class women, women who dressed or behaved like men, actresses, prostitutes, artists, writers, aristocrats, royalty (such as Marie Antoinette) or any woman with too much power could fall under suspicion of indulging in what a 1736 poem by William King called 'Lesbian loves'. So absolute ignorance of sexual possibilities between women cannot be assumed as a background to any of the poems in this anthology. Occasionally the polarized concepts of pure friendship and impure lust might even touch; the same pair of women (the Ladies of Llangollen, for example, discussed below) could be idealized as romantic friends *and* suspected of being 'damn'd Sapphists'.

Poetry, however, was a genteel genre that tended to ignore the ideas about 'Lesbian loves' circulating in grubbier texts such as newspapers, medical treatises and criminal biographies. In a huge body of lyric poetry, beginning in the mid-seventeenth century, women of the leisured classes wrote about their beloved friends usually under traditional pseudonyms (Lucasia, Ephelia, Ardelia), which preserved the friend's privacy and placed their love in a respectable literary tradition.

Many historians use the phrase 'romantic friendship' to imply that these extremely common pairings were non-sexual affections that have nothing at all in common with the contemporary concept of lesbianism. But it is hard to tell where these women drew the line between sensuality and sex, given that standard romantic-friend behaviour included sleeping together and pillowing your head on your beloved's bosom. Romantic friendship can be best thought of, I suggest, not as a particular, sexless kind of love but as a set of literary conventions for expressing love.

This anthology begins in Britain after the Restoration of Charles II, at a time of relative freedom, when serious numbers of women began to publish their work. Katherine Philips, 'the divine Orinda', is the founding mother of women's love poetry. Her 'To Mrs M. A., Upon Absence' (1664) is a classic poem of complaint while apart: 'Kept from thy face, link'd to thy heart'. Her 'To Rosania' (1664) is even more interesting, because the pain is caused not by absence but by frustrating nearness to the woman who cannot fully return her love. 'To My Excellent

Lucasia' (1664) idealizes women's 'innocent' love and grants it a status above marriage. In these poems Philips draws not only on the rhetoric of romantic friendship but also on the conventions of heterosexual passion found in the poetry of, say, John Donne.

Aphra Behn's few poems of passion for women are peculiarly daring and ambiguous. Like Philips, she uses heterosexual conventions; 'Verses design'd by Mrs A. Behn to be sent to a fair Lady, that desir'd she would absent herself to cure her Love. Left unfinish'd' (1692) is a classic poem of tortured love that could sound like a man addressing a woman except for the fact that Behn's rather in-your-face title makes the genders clear. In the much anthologized 'To the Fair Clarinda, Who Made Love to Me, Imagin'd More than Woman' (1688), the speaker plays with the common image from medical books of the lesbian as hermaphrodite.

> In pity to our Sex sure thou wert sent,
> That we might Love, and yet be Innocent:
> For sure no Crime with thee we can commit;
> Or if we shou'd – thy Form excuses it.
> For who, that gathers fairest Flowers believes
> A Snake lies hid beneath the Fragrant Leaves.

Here Behn slyly undermines her society's insistence on the 'Innocent' nature of women's love and suggests that there may be a criminal 'Snake' of desire hidden beneath the 'Fragrant Leaves' of romantic friendship.

Romantic Friendship: Eighteenth-century Contradictions

Moving into the eighteenth century, as middle-class women were pushed out of the trades and professions one by one and relegated to a life of feminine idleness, romantic friendship grew into a cult. Men sang its praises in their novels; women (whose literacy had increased enormously) became avid readers and writers on this theme. Poetry was seen as a suitably polite and unambitious genre for women, and just about every woman who published a slim collection in the eighteenth century included poems of 'love' or 'friendship' (using the two terms alternately) for women.

Most of them followed the divinely virtuous Katherine Philips rather than the scandalous playwright Aphra Behn. Philips's triumphalism in 'To My Excellent Lucasia' (1664) is clearly echoed by Anne Finch's 'Friendship between Ephelia and Ardelia' (1713). Generally the eighteenth-century poets do not reveal any of Aphra Behn's awareness of sexual possibilities between women; as writers anxious to maintain their respectability in a censorious age, they could not have risked such games. Eroticism, where it surfaces in this poetry, is subtle and gentle; for instance, Anne Finch in 'The White Mouses Petition' (written before 1720) speaks as a mouse who enjoys 'soft caresses' in the beloved's bosom, unnoticed by any 'jealous lover'.

Like many cults, romantic friendship was full of contradictions. For example, most romantic friends had husbands and saw the two relationships as highly compatible. But there were also strong associations between romantic friendship and spinsterhood (which peaked around 1725, when a quarter of the daughters of the landed gentry were unmarried). 'Spinster' had become a derogatory word by 1719, but many women writers fought back, boasting of the joys of single life. An anonymous magazine verse of 1720, 'Cloe to Artimesa', features a pair of women who share the exquisite 'Pleasures' of friendship, expressing scorn for 'tyrant' men as either husbands or lovers. It seems, then, that romantic friendship did not always back up marriage and the status quo.

One common poetic form was a contrast between men's love and women's. The Ladies of Llangollen, two upper-class Irishwomen who eloped to Wales in 1778, had become role models for virtuous female friendship; in 1789 the younger, Sarah Ponsonby, wrote a 'Song' that contrasts the terrors of erotic passion with the serene relief of love between women. A crucial part of the Ladies' international reputation was their lifestyle of rural retirement in their little cottage and garden; they re-inforced the idea of women's love as an idyllic retreat from mercenary, worldly, urban life. This pastoral setting is echoed in many of these poems, such as Charlotte MacCarthy's 'Content-ment, to a Friend' (1745) and Georgiana Spencer's 'To Lady Elizabeth Foster' (written in 1796).

This image of women off playing in the woods might seem harmless, but it contains a strong hint of separatism. If the Ladies of Llangollen had started a craze for women actually running away together rather than merely dreaming of it, they would not have been so respectable. In reality, almost all women lacked the money and opportunity to live with their beloved friends. One of the best examples of the enormous gap between real life and the pastoral dream is Eliza Robertson's 'A Poetical Epistle to an Absent Friend' (1801); this detailed plan for a blissful Llangollen-style life was actually written from Huntingdon jail.

Robertson is typical of the eighteenth-century poets in look-ing on the bright side. Unlike Philips and Behn, they tended not to emphasize the agonies inherent to love; they cast anxiety and pain as invasions from the outside, caused by enforced absence, sickness, death and breakdowns in communication. We can sense a certain defensiveness, perhaps a need to prove to society the perfection of women's love.

Considering that life expectancy in England in 1700 was about thirty-five, and lower for childbearing women, it makes sense that the elegy was a very popular form, as was the poem anticipating someone's death (see Mary Masters's 'To the Same; Enquiring Why I Wept', written in 1733). These poets tended to make a virtue of necessity, seeing death as a test or purifica-tion of love; moving examples include Jane Barker's 'On the Death of my Dear Friend' (1688) and two elegies by Elizabeth Singer Rowe, which speculate about whether women's love will live on in heaven.

Another reality of romantic friendship is that though women

paid each other long visits, sometimes even going on each other's honeymoons, their daily interaction usually consisted of writing or waiting for letters. Absence is a good condition for poetry; the beloved needs to be conjured up in words. Elizabeth Teft's 'On a Friend's taking a Journey' (1747) is practical and cheerful, but many poems express the frustration and boredom of life without the beloved; Elizabeth Hands's 'An Epistle' (1789) creates a disturbing picture of a woman who has literally nothing to do but pine for her friend. Given the vagaries of circumstance and the postal system, it is not surprising that breakdowns in communication seem to have been common. Mary Mollineux's 'Another Letter to a Friend' (1702) is one of the many letter-poems about the 'Doubtings' caused by a hiatus in correspondence. Here is another of the contradictions of romantic friendship; it was meant to be lofty and non-possessive, but many poems suggest a more troubled and jealous sort of love. In theory, women could have several romantic friends at once, and some did, but certain poems, such as Elizabeth Thomas's 'To Clemena' (1722), suggest rather a series of break-ups and new attachments, rather like serial monogamy.

In the latter half of the eighteenth century, literature was marked by a wallowing in emotion, a pre-Romantic cult of sensibility and hyper-sensitivity. One early example is Charlotte Lennox's 'Ardelia to Flavia, an Epistle' (1747); this frenzied account of a fight is unusual in its confession that the speaker was the one at fault for her paranoid 'Distrust' of the beloved. More often, poems take the point of view of the justifiably jealous or brokenhearted ex-friend. Susanna Highmore Duncombe's 'To Aspasia' (*c.* 1751), for instance, praises the love of women over the love of men, but undercuts this by going through a litany of 'unfaithful friends'. Notable in this tradition is Anna Seward's famous sequence of sonnets to Honora Sneyd (written in the 1770s), whom she considered had betrayed her by getting married; her 'Sonnet XXXI' is one of the few poems to admit to jealousy of a man.

Private Moments: Nineteenth-century Visions

As we move into the nineteenth century, there is no clear shift; women's romantic friendship continued to be celebrated in poetry. What we can detect is a subtle variation on eighteenth-century conventions, a certain turning inward, a new sense of the private.

In 1807 Sydney Owenson wrote of her first meeting with Mrs Lefanu; in 1867 Dora Greenwell devoted two sonnets to her single meeting with Elizabeth Barrett Browning. Women's love begins to sound fragmentary, a matter of precious fleeting moments rather than a solid social alliance. Barrett Browning addressed two passionate sonnets to George Sand in 1844, eight years before they would meet in person. We begin to get a sense of women's love as disembodied, and of literature as the space in which women 'met'.

It is significant that Barrett Browning addresses Sand as 'my sister'; Victorian women poets often dramatized their feminist solidarity with other women. Emily Hickey's 'For Richer, For Poorer' (1889) combines and rewrites the Bible stories of Ruth and Naomi and the Wise and Foolish Virgins

> . . . 'My oil is thine; for weal, for woe,
>   We two are one, and where thou goest I go,
>   One lot being ours for aye, where'er it lies.'

Whereas eighteenth-century poets of romantic friendship tend to refer to heaven rather vaguely, many nineteenth-century poets call on God personally. In some poems we sense a growing need to legitimate women's love as sacred. For example, Margaret Fuller's poem 'To A. H. B.' (written in 1836) attempts to rise above mere friendship; the speaker tells her friend that though they dream of some 'Elysium', some 'isle far from the haunts of men', the truth is that absence will ennoble them, 'that fire the gold should test'.

The greedy confidence that marks eighteenth-century

romantic-friendship poetry here begins to give way to a wearier, more resigned tone. Absence is no longer a circumstantial annoyance but part of the friends' destiny. Crucial here is Dorothy Wordsworth's 'Irregular Verses' (written 1827, left unfinished), written to the daughter of the friend from whom she has long been separated by their different duties. Unlike her eighteenth-century forebears, Wordsworth speaks in melancholy retrospect; the cottage she and her friend once longed to share is a romantic vision rather than a dream worth fighting for. Similarly, Dorothea Primrose Campbell's poem to an old school-friend, 'To Miss Sophia Headle' (1816), conjures up the lost pastoral landscape of their schooldays in Scotland but seems to assume that they will never meet again. The river that Caroline Clive describes in 'The Mosel' (1840) represents a single day away from real life in which she and her friend were free to be together. Helen Hunt Jackson's 'Friends' (1892) carries the same basic message of 'love will survive' as Eliza Cobbe's brisk 'To a Friend, Fearful of being Forgotten in Absence' (1796) but has a quite different, poignant tone; the distance itself has become romantic.

Death, of course, is the ultimate absence, and Victorian poetry thrived on it. Emily Dickinson is known for her death poems, but we also find interesting work by her English contemporaries, such as Bessie Rayner Parkes's 'Dream Fears' (1854), which is an attempt to deal with her dread of the beloved's death. Christina Rossetti's 1850s elegies, such as 'Gone Before' and 'Echo', put a new emphasis on the slipperiness, the untouchability, of the beloved even when alive; death seems part of the very character of these disembodied objects of Victorian desire.

Eighteenth-century writers, while upholding the ideal of pure love among educated, leisured women, had never denied the existence of female sexuality; the myth of the asexual woman was an early-nineteenth-century creation. In an 1811 libel case two Scottish schoolteachers were accused of 'lewd and indecent behaviour'; most of their judges, however, insisted that British women were neither physically nor morally capable of such things. This climate of denial, paradoxically, allowed the occasional expression of overwhelming sensuality in poetry. Alice Cary's 'The Window Just Over the Street' (written before 1871) is the story of a depressed woman who cheers up when she looks across the street and sees a beautiful girl undressing. It is an astonishing piece of voyeurism, but it sounds as if it was written in all innocence by an author who never suspected that she might be writing about sexual desire.

Crucially, Cary's poem is about a vision; in Victorian poetry women's love more often inhabits a place of private, fantastical daydreams than the everyday social world. In Mary Russell Mitford's 'Written in a Blank-Paper Book Given to the Author by a Friend' (1827), the blank book stands for the beloved and conjures up a hallucination of her, 'a vision of delight'. Frances Kemble's 'A Noonday Vision' (1866) is more of a nightmare, as the beloved teeters on a precipice. In Dora Greenwell's moving 'Reconciliation' (1861), a woman alienated from her friend for many years dreams that they are blissfully reconciled.

Even pastoral poems in the nineteenth century are marked by this sense of the private, the visionary. In Anne Grant's 'The Nymph of the Fountain to Charlotte' (1803) the lover speaks as the feminine spirit of the water that gets to wash the beloved's body; this is no open field, but a hidden, secluded place. Secret gardens are common; sometimes they are entirely symbolic, as in Frances Osgood's 'The Garden of Friendship' (1850), which uses traditional Victorian flower imagery to cast the beloved as the unique 'queen-rose'.

Emily Dickinson's poems to women make more sense when read against this backdrop. Many of her poems read like hallucinatory visions; the garden in 'Baffled for just a day or two' and the harbour in 'Wild Nights – Wild Nights!' are just two of her secret places. In 'Her breast is fit for pearls' (written about 1859) we get the sense that the dreamed-of cottage of female love has become completely internalized.

> Her heart is fit for *home* –
> I – a Sparrow – build there
> Sweet of twigs and twine
> My perennial nest.

But there is nothing cosy about Dickinson's sense of love between women. Consider this enigmatic challenge, in 'I showed her Heights she never saw' (written about 1862):

> I showed her Secrets – Morning's Nest –
> The Rope the Nights were put across –
> And *now* – 'Would'st have me for a Guest?'
> She could not find her Yes –

Telling Secrets: The Transitional Generations

Towards the end of the nineteenth century the word 'secret' begins to show up quite often in poems between women. Rosa Mulholland's 'A Stolen Visit' (1886) is in one way a classic Victorian poem of disembodied friendship, but it has an oddly covert quality, as the speaker imagines creeping round the beloved's house at night, sighing over everything she has used or touched; 'My love hath left no mark behind', she ends, with a hint of guilt that strikes a new note in women's love poetry. Even more enigmatic is A. Mary F. Robinson's 'Rosa Rosarum' (1886), in which the red rose the two girls throw down the well becomes a symbol for a secret they share, the source of their intimacy, something that will never rise to 'shame' them.

What unites the writers I group under the heading of the transitional generations – roughly, 1870–1914 – is that they were writing during a period of metamorphosis in society's view of what love between women could mean. Karl Westphal in 1869 was the first of the European 'sexologists' to give extensive discussion to the idea of lesbians as, to put it simply, men in women's bodies; he was followed by Richard von Krafft-Ebing and Havelock Ellis, and by the 1890s debates were raging over what we now call sexual orientation. After centuries of haphazard and unofficial discussion of same-sex possibilities, passion between women was being classified under such labels as 'inversion', 'perversion', 'contrary sexuality' and 'uranism'; the 'homosexual' and then the 'heterosexual' were invented as opposite types. On the one hand, this moment pathologized lesbianism, associating it with violence, congenital defects and insanity; on the other, it did bring it into the light. For many reasons, however, this 'new knowledge' did not spread very fast; it had to combat disbelief and social inertia. (As the story goes, Victoria's ministers wanted to extend the anti-sodomy laws to cover women, but the Queen could not be persuaded that there was any such thing as lesbianism.) From the 1890s stories of 'inversion' did begin showing up in the public debating chambers of fiction and theatre but almost never in poetry.

Meanwhile, with the growth in education and professions for women – by 1880 every third student in higher education was a woman – more and more women found it possible actually to live together. In late-nineteenth-century American cities, female domestic partnerships were so common that they became known as 'Boston marriages'. Despite the slow leakage of the sexological theories into public awareness, then, a confident breed of educated women continued to write love poetry to women. For all the continuity, though, we begin to hear a questioning of the codes of Victorian romantic friendship. In Florence Converse's pair of sonnets on 'Friendship' (1897), we see the speaker struggling with the Shakespearian-sonnet tradition of romantic same-sex passion, worrying that it is too selfish for these duty-bound times. This demanding sort of love would come to dominate women's poetry; the tide was turning against Florence Converse and her like. Another poem in the form of a debate with the self, Sophie Jewett's 'A Letter' (1896) to her absent friend, shows the Victorian code of stoical absence crumbling;

> Forgive me if I tell myself in vain:
> 'There is no power in this wide world to part
> Our souls. Avail not time nor space nor pain,
> For love is unconditioned.' Dear, to-night,
> I am like an unlessoned child, who cries
> For the sweet sensual things of touch and sight;

Those who followed Jewett would concentrate more and more on the 'sweet sensual things'; the tendency, in line with heterosexuality's own changes at the time, was towards overwhelming romance.

Something that seems distinctly new in the poetry of the transitional generations is gendered role-play. In romantic friendship poetry the two women are usually described in a symmetrical way. But now poets began to play with personae, increasing the contrast between lover and beloved. The object of love in these poems is almost always described in traditionally feminine terms: flower, lady, queen. For the lover sometimes a masculine persona is adopted, sometimes the lover's gender is left unclear and sometimes she takes on the literary role of page, troubadour, poet or subordinate worshipper. In Violet Fane's 'At Her Feet' (1880) the speaker is self-consciously reproducing an old book's pose, as the page in love with the lady (who thinks only of another man). Isa Blagden's 'Alice' (1873) is more explicit about what it means to be 'true to ancient fashion'.

> I, a page, a servant,
>   Alice as a queen
> At my love so fervent
>   Smiles, with pride serene.

This kind of love, Blagden makes quite clear, is one-way:

> Wine poured from a chalice
>   Flows not back again.

More happily, in Mary Coleridge's 'Regina' (1896), the poet speaker is intimately necessary to the beloved 'Queen'. This role-play can operate in a modern setting too; in Amy Levy's wistful 'To Lallie' (1884), set in Cambridge and London, Lallie and the ungendered speaker who punts her down the river are opposed as 'rosebud maiden' and 'poet', 'tyrant' and 'slave' respectively. The beloved is not always a noble queen; several of these poems, such as Angelina Weld Grimké's 'Caprichosa' (written in 1901), reveal her to be a flirt, and remind us that no matter how humble the poet's pose, the power of judgement is always in her hands.

This kind of gendered role-play is noticeable in women's love poetry from the 1870s, long before the sexologists' theories were widely publicized. It seems most likely that it was an adaptation of heterosexual conventions – and Pre-Raphaelite imagery in particular – to give new life, and more dramatic force, to poems of love between women. This sense of liberating role-play is made explicitly erotic in Mathilde Blind's 'A Fantasy' (1895), in which a woman describes fantasizing about being an Arab man and feeling 'parched with desire' for a woman. In a poem written by the vaudeville male impersonator Annie Hindle, 'Her Gift' (1871), the speaker who teases the girl until finally winning the fetishized kiss is not identified as a man or a woman but is marked as masculine in behaviour. This is a perfect example of encoding by a lesbian poet; published in a newspaper, 'Her Gift' was probably read at the time as being about a man and a woman, though now it seems highly suggestive of the evolution of butch/femme roles in the late nineteenth century.

A masculine or androgynous persona, however, was not compulsory. Other poetry of the 1890s shows quite a lot of erotic freedom; see, for instance, Helen Hunt Jackson's 'Her Eyes' (1892) and Annie Fields's 'To ——, Sleeping' (1895), which shows one woman looking at another's cheek, 'our home of kisses'. Occasionally we catch a glimpse of lesbian love as sin or perversity, which was much more common in French and German poetry than in the English language. Helen Hay Whitney's 1905 series of sonnets, for instance, makes occasional allusion to the nineteenth-century European tradition of lesbian decadence:

> Violent sin
> Blazed me a path, and I have walked therein,
> Strong, unashamed.

But even though she invokes 'sin', her speaker resists 'shame'. There is surprisingly little in women's poetry of the note we hear in Lord Alfred Douglas's 1894 poem on the love 'that dare not speak its name'. Angelina Weld Grimké's undated poem 'Rosabel' suggests that the speaker does not 'dare' to speak her love to the beloved, but she ends the poem by declaring it to the reader; the tone is more one of coy, delighted secrecy than of weighty shame.

The transitional generations include several confident and fascinating poets whose virtues I can only touch on here. Much more work needs to be done on Mary Coleridge, for instance; she is particularly good on broken relationships and rewrites her great-great-uncle's poem 'Christabel' (1816), with much more direct focus on the forbidden desire, as 'The Witch' (1896). Another unjustly neglected poet is Amy Levy, whose 'At a Dinner Party' (1889) is a quiet laugh at the expense of a society in denial.

> You look across the fruit and flowers,
> My glance your glances find. –
> It is our secret, only ours,
> Since all the world is blind.

The prevalent sense of secrets to be told is noticeably absent from the work of that extraordinary couple who wrote as 'Michael Field'. Their book of rewritten fragments from Sappho in 1889 allowed them to begin writing frankly about sexual passion between women; they moved on to powerful lyrics about the sacramental quality of their daily love, their embrace of Roman Catholicism, their sicknesses and deaths. In their unabashed reconciliation of religion and lust, Victorian ethics and modern sensibilities, 'Michael Field' epitomizes this strange era of transition in love poetry between women.

Waking Up Together: Modern Love

Much that had been relatively constant in women's lives began to change during and after the First World War, and society's perception of love between women changed at a faster rate too. Though Boston-marriage-style partnerships never quite died out, it became more and more difficult to ignore the erotic possibilities; as Freud's theories were added to those of the early sexologists, suddenly sexuality (repressed or otherwise) was seen everywhere. Some found this liberating; lesbian sub-cultures bloomed in certain cities, notably Paris. Others reacted with anxiety, as in Katherine Mansfield's poem on 'Friendship' (1919):

> It's bigger than a Tiger,
>   Its eyes are jets of flame,
> Its claws are gleaming daggers,
>   Could it have once been tame?

One result of this new awareness was increased censorship. In 1926 a Broadway play with a lesbian theme, *The Captive*, led to the arrest of its cast. A major watershed was the 1928 trial of Radclyffe Hall's 'invert' novel, *The Well of Loneliness*, for 'obscene libel'. As usual, however, poetry was a different matter; the poems in this section of the anthology seem relatively untouched by the climate of tension in which they were written.

What we find in some, instead of the weighty *angst* of *The Well of Loneliness*, is a delicate melancholy characteristic of modernist literature. Charlotte Mew's ambiguously gendered narrators sound thwarted rather than guilty. H. D. sings the eroticism of frustration in 'At Baia' (1921):

> I send you this,
> who left the blue veins
> of your throat unkissed.

Titles become rather bolder; Edna St Vincent Millay explores jealousy in 'Evening on Lesbos' (1928), and Elizabeth Daryush tests the rules of 'Forbidden Love' (1934).

A much more common note in the poetry of the 1910s, 1920s and 1930s, however, is open longing for what Sophie Jewett in 1896 called 'the sweet sensual things of touch and sight'. 'Would that I were Sappho,' Lesbia Harford wrote in 1915, complaining of a chaste beloved. All those Victorian poems that make a virtue of absence seem to be answered by Amy Lowell's impatient desire in 'The Letter' (1919): 'I am tired, Beloved, of chafing my heart against/The want of you'. More and more, though, these poets wrote about presence rather than absence; there was a new sense that the details of everyday life were the stuff of love poetry. Lowell's long sequence 'Two Speak Together' (1919) was written ten years into a lesbian marriage; only the occasional masculine pronoun tried to mask this. Similarly, in New Zealand Ursula Bethell was writing unsentimental hymns of domestic life with her 'consort':

> The taste of the potatoes was satisfactory
> With a sprig of fresh mint, dairy butter, and very young
> > green peas.

Another powerful sequence of poems is Katharine Lee Bates's 'In Bohemia' (1922), a set of elegiac sonnets; it is the tiny things like the sound of the car that remind her of the dead beloved, 'sweet as daily bread,/Refreshing as cool water'.

More unusual as a body of work about a long-term partner-ship is the joint collection of poems published in 1934 by Sylvia Townsend Warner and Valentine Ackland; instead of emphasiz-ing peace and harmony, they focus on the storm, the elemental, disruptive power of their love. Similarly, a poem I did not get permission to publish, Elizabeth Bishop's 'It is marvellous to wake up together' (written in the 1940s but left unpublished) speaks of making love in an electrical storm; waking up together is a risky business. Another form of modernist rebellion against the happy-marriage mode is found in poems that question

monogamy; examples include Natalie Barney's 'Habit' (1920),
Vita Sackville-West's 'No Obligation' (1932) and the extraordi-
nary Elsa Gidlow's take on 'Constancy' (1923):

> You're jealous if I kiss this girl and that,
> You think I should be constant to one mouth?
> Little you know of my too quenchless drouth:
> My sister, I keep faith with love, not lovers.

The most obvious change in poetry of the 1910s, 1920s
and 1930s is a new openness about sex. Some continued to
play with puns and codes; Gertrude Stein hid outrageous pas-
sages in the middle of long poems like 'Lifting Belly' (written
1915–17):

> Lifting belly is so kind.
> Lifting belly fattily.
> Doesn't that astonish you.
> You did want me.
> Say it again.
> Strawberry.

In the 1920s Elsa Gidlow, Amy Lowell and H. D. wrote with a
more direct focus on desire. The first really explicit poem about
love-making in this anthology is Valentine Ackland's audacious
'The eyes of the body, being blindfold by night' (1934):

> My hand, being deft and delicate, displays
> Unerring judgment; cleaves between your thighs
> Clean, as a ray-directed airplane flies.

Rather strangely, this courage and clarity of vision seems to
fade at the end of the 1930s. Though some good poems from
the 1940s and 1950s are included here, they are generally veiled,
almost muted. Perhaps the social climate was making it more and
more difficult to write such poetry. Popular versions of Freud's
theories called passion between women a sign of arrested devel-
opment; witchhunts in such institutions as the US Army drove

it out. Lesbian culture thrived in the urban underworld of the bars now and was displayed in pulp fiction; not until the 1970s would it come alive in poetry again.

Dancing in the Dangerous World: Contemporary Questions

In the 1970s the Women's Movement and Gay Liberation together created a tidal wave in this poetic tradition. New theories – of the emotional, erotic and political value of female friendship and love, and Adrienne Rich's hypothesis of a 'lesbian continuum' of bonds between women – enabled the celebration of many kinds of love. We can sense this explosion of energy in most of the poems included here from the 1970s, 1980s and 1990s. What is less often pointed out is how much continuity there is between these poets and their forebears.

Many of them continued the project of finding moments of revelation in the banal domesticity of most women's lives. The bath-sharing lovers in Maureen Duffy's 'Eureka' (1971) know each other's bodies better than their own. Like Antoinette Scudder in the 1940s, Olga Broumas eroticizes a cup of tea in 'Song / for Sanna' (1977). Judy Grahn's 'Ah, Love, you smell of petroleum' (1977) ruefully contrasts the appleblossom and olive oil of romance with the reality of the daily grind, but ends 'we shall dance in the kitchen of our imagination'.

Many follow Valentine Ackland and Sylvia Townsend Warner by invoking elemental forces of nature to describe love-making; examples here include the sea in Suniti Namjoshi's and Gillian Hanscombe's 'Well, then let slip the masks' (1986), and the soaked landscape of Audre Lorde's classic 'Love Poem' (1971). The weather in Jackie Kay's 'Pounding Rain' (1991) suggests both erotic overflow and the risk these married women are taking in a small town where 'News of us spreads like a storm'. In poems by such writers as Minnie Bruce Pratt the movements of nature help to explain the seasons of love; the poem reprinted here from May Sarton's 'The Autumn Sonnets' (1972) describes what remains after loss, 'The strong root still alive under the snow'. Like their eighteenth-century forebears, many contemporary poets still turn to nature as the world in which women's love makes most sense.

There is a new honesty about painful issues of prejudice and conflict, the distances between us. Instead of blissful fusion, the focus is often the tricky dance of negotiation, as in May Swenson's startling sequence 'Poet to Tiger' (1970):

> You don't put salt on anything
>   so I'm eating without.
> Honey on the eggs is all right
>   mustard on the toast.
> I'm not complaining I'm saying I'm
>   living with *you*.

Marilyn Hacker catches the insecurity, the second-guessing of love affairs, in her stylish villanelle 'Coming Downtown' (1986). Hacker's lovers tend to inhabit a prickly urban environment; so does the speaker who fears the beloved's death in Naomi Replansky's 'The Dangerous World' (1994). More positively, there is a new celebration of the beloved's independence and ultimate unknowability found in Daphne Marlatt's joyous 'Coming to you' (1984), in which the speaker looks through a window at the beloved who is wearing headphones, 'rapt with inaudible music'. An even more poignant sense of separateness marks Jane Chambers's 'To Beth On Her Forty-Second Birthday' (published in 1984), which adapts an old pattern (a poem to the sleeping beloved) into a sort of inverse elegy, a farewell from the dying poet.

Many love poems between women nowadays head straight for the crotch – with ripe fruit, lush flowers and seaweed being particularly popular metaphors – as if making up for lost time. But it would be a shame to lose sight of all the other, and sometimes subtler, ways of speaking love; see, for instance, Carol

Ann Duffy's profoundly erotic 'Warming Her Pearls' (1987). The best contemporary poetry has a playfulness which I find heartening; Cheryl Clarke's bluesy 'Nothing' (1986) and Brenda Brooks's gleeful 'Anything' (1990) are both about juggling an infinity of roles.

Despite all the historical changes, then, the genre of poetry seems always to have represented a freer – perhaps because more private, veiled and metaphorical – space for the expression of love between women in all its variety. But though the poems gathered here benefit from being read as a coherent tradition, I have no case to make about the uniqueness of poems written by and for women. Love poetry at its best has always tended towards the universal, rushing past the who and what to get to the transcendental why.

Further Reading

Andreadis, Harriette, 'The Sapphic-Platonics of Katherine Philips, 1632–1664', *Signs*, 15:1 (1989), 34–60

Burford, Barbara, Lindsay MacRae and Sylvia Paskin (eds.), *Dancing the Tightrope: New Love Poems by Women* (London, 1987)

Coss, Clare (ed.), *The Arc of Love: An Anthology of Lesbian Love Poems* (New York, 1996)

Donoghue, Emma, *Passions Between Women: British Lesbian Culture, 1668–1801* (London, 1993)

Duberman, Martin, Martha Vicinus and George Chauncey (eds.), *Hidden from History: Reclaiming the Gay and Lesbian Past* (New York, 1989)

Faderman, Lillian, *Surpassing the Love of Men: Romantic Friendship and Love Between Women from the Renaissance to the Present* (New York, 1981)

——*Odd Girls and Twilight Lovers: A History of Lesbian Life in Twentieth-century America* (New York, 1991)

Faderman, Lillian (ed.), *Chloe Plus Olivia: An Anthology of Lesbian Literature from the Seventeenth Century to the Present* (New York, 1994)

Grahn, Judy, *The Highest Apple: Sappho and the Lesbian Poetic Tradition* (San Francisco, 1985)

Greer, Germaine, and others (eds.), *Kissing the Rod: An Anthology of Seventeenth-century Women's Verse* (London, 1988)

Griffin, Gabriele, *Heavenly Love? Lesbian Images in Twentieth-century Women's Writing* (Manchester, 1993)

Hobby, Elaine, and Chris White (eds.), *What Lesbians Do in Books* (London, 1991)

Jay, Karla, and Joanne Glasgow (eds.), *Lesbian Texts and Contexts: Radical Revisions* (New York, 1990)

Kehoe, Monika (ed.), *Historical, Literary and Erotic Aspects of Lesbianism* (New York, 1986)

Landry, Donna, *The Muses of Resistance: Labouring-Class Women's Poetry in Britain, 1739–1796* (Cambridge, 1990)

Larkin, Joan, and Carl Morse (eds.), *Gay and Lesbian Poetry in Our Time: An Anthology* (New York, 1988)

Leighton, Angela, and Margaret Reynolds (eds.), *Victorian Women Poets: An Anthology* (Oxford, 1995)

Lonsdale, Roger (ed.), *Eighteenth-Century Women Poets: An Oxford Anthology* (Oxford, 1989)

Malinowski, Sharon, and Christa Brelin (eds.), *The Gay and Lesbian Literary Companion* (Detroit, 1995)

Mavor, Elizabeth, *The Ladies of Llangollen: A Study in Romantic Friendship* (London, 1971)

McEwen, Christian (ed.), *Naming the Waves: Contemporary Lesbian Poetry* (London, 1988)

Mohin, Lilian (ed.), *Beautiful Barbarians: Lesbian Feminist Poetry* (London, 1986)

Moore, Lisa, 'Something More Tender Still than Friendship: Romantic Friendship in Early-Nineteenth-Century England', *Feminist Studies*, 18:3 (1992), 499–520

Mulford, Wendy (ed.), *The Virago Book of Love Poetry* (London, 1990)

Newman, Lesléa (ed.), *My Lover is a Woman: Contemporary Lesbian Love Poems* (New York, 1996)

Raitt, Suzanne (ed.), *Volcanoes and Pearl-divers: Lesbian Feminist Studies*, (London, 1995)

Raymond, Janice, *A Passion for Friends: Towards a Philosophy of Female Affection* (London, 1986)

Smith-Rosenberg, Carroll, 'The Female World of Love and Ritual: Relations Between Women in Nineteenth-century America', *Signs*, 1:1 (1975), 1–29

Todd, Janet, *Women's Friendship in Literature* (New York, 1980)

Todd, Janet (ed.), *A Dictionary of British and American Women Writers 1660–1800* (London, 1987)

Van Casselaer, Catherine, *Lot's Wife: Lesbian Paris, 1890–1914* (Liverpool, 1986)

White, Chris, '"Poets and Lovers Evermore": Interpreting Female Love in the Poetry and Journals of Michael Field', *Textual Practice*, 4:2 (1990), 197–212

Katherine Philips

(ENGLAND AND WALES, 1631–64)

To Mrs M. A., Upon Absence

'Tis now since I began to die
   Four months and more, yet gasping live;
Wrapp'd up in sorrows do I lie,
   Hoping, yet doubting a reprieve.
Adam from Paradise expell'd
Just such a wretched being held.

'Tis not thy love I fear to lose,
   That will in spite of absence hold;
But 'tis the benefit and use
   Is lost, as in imprison'd Gold:
Which though the sum be ne'er so great,
Enriches nothing but conceit.

What angry star then governs me
   That I must feel a double smart?
Pris'ner to fate as well as thee;
   Kept from thy face, link'd to thy heart?
Because my love all Love excells,
Must my griefs have no parallels?

Sapless and dead as winter here
   I now remain, and all I see
Copies of my wild 'state appear,
   But I am their epitomy.
Love me no more! for I am grown
Too dead and dull for thee to own.

(wr. 1650, pub. 1664)

To Rosania (now Mrs Mountague) being with her, 25th September 1652

As men that are with visions grac'd
Must have all other thoughts displac'd,
And buy those short descents of Light
With loss of sense, and spirit's flight:

So since thou wert my happiness,
I could not hope the rate was less;
And thus the vision which I gain
Is short t'enjoy, and hard t'attain.

Ah! what a trifle then is all
That thing which here we pleasure call!
Since what our very soul hath cost
Is hardly got, and quickly lost.

Yet there is Justice in the fate;
For should we dwell in blest estate,
Our Joys thereby would so inflame,
We should forget from whence they came.

If this so sad a doom can quit
Me for the follies I commit;
Let no estrangement on thy part
Add a new ruin to my heart.

When on my self I do reflect,
I can no smile from thee expect:
But if thy kindness hath no plea,
Some freedom grant for Charity.

Else the Just world must needs deny
Our friendship an Eternity:
This love will ne'er that title hold;
For mine's too hot, and thine too cold.

Divided Rivers lose their name;
And so our too unequal flame
Parted, will passion be in me,
And an indifference in thee.

Thy absence I could easier find
Provided thou wert well, and kind,
Than such a presence as this is,
Made up of snatches of my bliss.

So when the Earth long gasps for rain,
If she at last some few drops gain,
She is more parched than at first;
That small recruit increased the Thirst.

(wr. 1652, pub. 1664)

To My Excellent Lucasia, On Our Friendship

I did not live until this time
    Crown'd my felicity,
When I could say without a crime,
    I am not Thine, but Thee.

This Carcass breath'd, and walk'd, and slept,
    So that the world believ'd
There was a soul the motions kept;
    But they were all deceiv'd.

For as a watch by art is wound
    To motion, such was mine;
But never had Orinda found
    A Soul till she found thine;

Which now inspires, cures and supplies,
    And guides my darken'd breast:
For thou art all that I can prize,
    My Joy, my Life, my rest.

No bridegroom's nor crown'd conqu'rour's mirth
    To mine compar'd can be:
They have but pieces of this Earth,
    I've all the world in thee.

Then let our flame still light and shine
    (And no bold fear control),
As innocent as our design,
    Immortal as our Soul.

(wr. 1651, pub. 1664)

Aphra Behn

(ENGLAND, DUTCH GUIANA AND THE NETHERLANDS, 1640–89)

To the Fair Clarinda, Who Made Love to Me, Imagin'd More than Woman

Fair lovely Maid, or if that Title be
Too weak, too Feminine for Nobler thee,
Permit a Name that more Approaches Truth:
And let me call thee, Lovely Charming Youth.
This last will justify my soft complaint,
While that may serve to lessen my constraint;
And without Blushes I the Youth pursue,
When so much beauteous Woman is in view.
Against thy Charms we struggle but in vain
With thy deluding Form thou giv'st us pain,
While the bright Nymph betrays us to the Swain.

In pity to our Sex sure thou wert sent,
That we might Love, and yet be Innocent:
For sure no Crime with thee we can commit;
Or if we shou'd – thy Form excuses it.
For who, that gathers fairest Flowers believes
A Snake lies hid beneath the Fragrant Leaves.

Thou beauteous Wonder of a different kind,
Soft *Cloris* with the dear *Alexis* join'd;*
When e'r the Manly part of thee, wou'd plead
Thou tempts us with the Image of the Maid,
While we the noblest Passions do extend
The Love to *Hermes, Aphrodite* the Friend.†

(1688)

To My Lady Morland at Tunbridge

As when a Conqu'ror does in Triumph come,
And proudly leads the vanquish'd Captives home,
The Joyful People crowd in ev'ry Street,
And with loud shouts of Praise the Victor greet;
While some whom Chance or Fortune kept away,
Desire at least the Story of the Day;
How brave the Prince, how gay the Chariot was,
How beautiful he look'd, with what a Grace;
Whether upon his Head he Plumes did wear;
Or if a Wreath of Bays adorn'd his Hair:
They hear 'tis wondrous fine, and long much more
To see the Hero than they did before.

* Cloris and Alexis: common names in pastoral poetry for a nymph (woman)
and a swain (man).
† Hermes and Aphrodite: the parents of Hermaphroditus, the boy who
became of one body with the nymph Salmacis, producing the word
'hermaphrodite'.

So when the Marvels by Report I knew,
Of how much Beauty, *Cloris*, dwelt in you;
How many Slaves your Conqu'ring Eyes had won,
And how the gazing Crowd admiring throng:
I wish'd to see, and much a Lover grew
Of so much Beauty, though my Rival too.
I came and saw, and blessed my Destiny;
I found it Just you should out-Rival me.
'Twas at the Altar, where more Hearts were giv'n
To you that day, than were address'd to Heav'n.
The Rev'rend Man whose Age and Mystery
Had rendred Youth and Beauty Vanity,
By fatal Chance casting his Eyes your way,
Mistook the duller Bus'ness of the Day,
Forgot the Gospel, and began to Pray.
Whilst the Enamour'd Crowd that near you pressed,
Receiving Darts which none could e'er resist,
Neglected the Mistake o' th' Love-sick Priest.
Ev'n my Devotion, *Cloris*, you betray'd,
And I to Heaven no other Petition made,
But that you might all other Nymphs out-do
In Cruelty as well as Beauty too.
I call'd *Amyntas* Faithless Swain before,
But now I find 'tis Just he should Adore.
Not to love you, a wonder sure would be,
Greater than all his Perjuries to me.
And whilst I Blame him, I Excuse him too;
Who would not venture Heav'n to purchase you?
But Charming *Cloris*, you too meanly prize
The more deserving Glories of your Eyes,
If you permit him on an Amorous score,
To be your Slave, who was my Slave before.
He oft has Fetters worn, and can with ease
Admit 'em or dismiss 'em when he please.

A Virgin-Heart you merit, that ne'er found
It could receive, till from your Eyes, the Wound;
A Heart that nothing but your Force can fear,
And own a Soul as Great as you are Fair.

(1684)

Verses design'd by Mrs A. Behn to be sent to a fair Lady, that desir'd she would absent herself to cure her Love. Left unfinish'd.

In vain to Woods and Deserts I retire,
To shun the lovely Charmer I admire,
Where the soft Breezes do but fan my Fire!
In vain in Grottos dark unseen I lie,
Love pierces where the Sun could never spy.
No place, no Art his Godhead can exclude,
The Dear Distemper reigns in Solitude:
Distance, alas, contributes to my Grief;
No more, of what fond Lovers call, Relief
Than to the wounded Hind does sudden Flight
From the chaste Goddess's* pursuing Sight:
When in the Heart the fatal Shaft remains,
And darts the Venom through our bleeding Veins.
If I resolve no longer to submit
My self a wretched Conquest to your Wit,
More swift than fleeting Shades, ten thousand Charms
From your bright Eyes that Rebel Thought disarms:
The more I struggl'd, to my Grief I found
My self in *Cupid*'s Chains more surely bound:
Like Birds in Nets, the more I strive, I find
My self the faster in the Snare confin'd.

(1692)

* chaste Goddess: Diana, goddess of the forest, the hunt and maidens.

Mary Mollineux

(ENGLAND, *c.* 1651–95)

Another Letter to a Friend

My hasty Pen, about to write Unkind,
(When interrupted by my zealous Mind)
Again admits of dear *Marcaria*; tho'
Thy tedious Silence gives affront unto
True Cordial Friendship, which in ev'ry State
Sweetly delighteth to communicate
Pure Streams of Love, as opportunity
Permits, to manifest its Sympathy:
Which, seeming now to cease, gives cause of doubt,
Some new Concern hath jostled Friendship out
From that fair Bosom; where, if yet it dwell,
'Twill by its influencing Power dispel
Whate'er would stop its Current: For we see
That standing Pools oft-times corrupted be,
When smaller Brooks, whose Streams do gently glide
Along their Banks, are purg'd and purify'd.
Alas, that Love that burns with fervency,
Is frequently perplexed with Jealousy!
Then why so Silent? Why so strangely Mute?
Must I indeed not only find my Suit
Ungranted, but Disdain'd? And must I be
Therefore unanswer'd, for a Penalty
To be impos'd, as for a heinous Crime?
Tho' I forgot once a Request of thine,
I did not wholly throw aside my Pen;
But, as full fraught with other matter, when
In hopes of sending, though I did omit
To answer each Punctilio, yet I writ,

(Grateful or not:) For my Officious Quill,
As formerly engag'd, is ready still
To write to thee. –
Ah! Canst thou think what Doubtings do attend,
Whether sad Sickness, or some rival Friend
May now so long restrain thy careless Pen,
As if it would not deign to write again?
Or must that Friendship in Oblivion lie,
That seems Immortal? Then send Reasons why:
How should I else resent this Injury?

(1702)

Jane Barker

(ENGLAND AND FRANCE, 1652–*c*. 1727)

On the Death of my Dear Friend and Play-fellow, Mrs E. D. having Dream'd the night before I heard thereof, that I had lost a Pearl

I Dream'd I lost a Pearl, and so it prov'd;
I lost a Friend much above Pearls belov'd:
A Pearl perhaps adorns some outward part,
But Friendship decks each corner of the heart:
Friendship's a Gem, whose Lustre do's out-shine
All that's below the heav'nly Crystaline:
Friendship is that mysterious thing alone,
Which can unite, and make two Hearts but one;
It purifies our Love, and makes it flow,
I' th' clearest stream that's found in Love below;
It sublimates the Soul, and makes it move
Towards Perfection and Celestial Love.

We had no by-designs, nor hop'd to get
Each by the other place amongst the great;
Not Riches hop'd, nor Poverty we fear'd,
'Twas Innocence in both, which both rever'd.
Witness this truth the Wilsthorp-Fields, where we
So oft enjoy'd a harmless Luxury;
Where we indulg'd our easie Appetites,
With Pocket-Apples, Plumbs, and such delights:
Then we contriv'd to spend the rest o' th' day,
In making Chaplets, or at Check-stone play;
When weary, we our selves supinely laid
On Beds of Violets under some cool shade,
Where th' Sun in vain strove to dark through his Rays,
Whilst Birds around us chanted forth their Lays;
Ev'n those we had bereaved of their young,
Would greet us with a Querimonious* Song.
Stay here, my Muse, and of these let us learn,
The loss of our deceased Friend to Mourn:
Learn did I say? alas, that cannot be,
We can teach Clouds to weep, and Winds to sigh at Sea,
Teach Brooks to murmur, Rivers to o'er-flow,
We can add Solitude to Shades of Yew.
Were Turtles to be witness of our moan,
They'd in compassion quite forget their own:
Nor shall hereafter *Heraclitus*† be,
Fam'd for his Tears, but to my Muse and Me;
Fate shall give all that Fame can comprehend,
Ah poor repair for th' loss of such a Friend.

(1688)

---

* querimonious: querulous, peevish.
† Heraclitus: Heraclitus of Ephesus (writing *c.* 500 BC) was called the
'weeping philosopher' because of his conviction that nothing lasts.

Anne Killigrew

(ENGLAND, 1660–85)

On the Soft and Gentle Motions of Eudora

Divine Thalia* strike th' Harmonious Lute,
But with a Stroke so Gentle as may suit
The silent gliding of the Hours,
Or yet the calmer growth of Flowers;
Th' ascending or the falling Dew,
Which none can see, though all find true.
    For thus alone,
    Can be shown,
  How downy, how smooth
  Eudora doth Move,
How Silken her Actions appear,
  The Air of her Face,
  Of a gentler Grace
Than those that do stroke the Ear.
  Her Address so sweet,
  So Modestly Meet,†
That 'tis not the Loud though Tuneable String,
Can show forth so soft, so Noiseless a Thing!
  O This to express from thy Hand must fall,
  Than Music's self, something more Musical.

(1686)

* Thalia: one of the Muses who inspires pastoral poetry.
† meet: fitting.

Anne Finch, Countess of Winchilsea

(ENGLAND, 1661–1720)

Friendship between Ephelia and Ardelia*

EPHELIA   What Friendship is, Ardelia, show.
ARDELIA   'Tis to love as I love you.
EPHELIA   This account, so short (though kind),
          Suits not my inquiring mind.
          Therefore farther now repeat:
          What is Friendship when complete?
ARDELIA   'Tis to share all joy and grief;
          'Tis to lend all due relief
          From the tongue, the heart, the hand;
          'Tis to mortgage house and land;
          For a friend be sold a slave;
          'Tis to die upon a grave,
          If a friend therein do lie.
EPHELIA   This indeed, though carried high;
          This though more then e'er was done
          Underneath the rolling sun,
          This has all been said before.
          Can Ardelia say no more?
ARDELIA   Words indeed no more can show:
          But 'tis to love, as I love you.

(1713)

* Ardelia: the name Anne Finch adopted for literary matters.

The White Mouses Petition to Lamira the Right Honble the Lady Anne Tufton now Countess of Salisbury

With all respect and humble duty
And passing every mouse in Beauty
With far more white than garden lillies
And eyes as bright as any Phillis*
I sue to wear Lamira's fetters
And live the envy of my betters
When I receive her soft caresses
And creeping near her lovely tresses
Their glossy brown from my reflection
Shall gain more lustre and perfection
And to her bosom if admitted
My colour there will be so fitted
That no distinction cou'd discover
My station to a jealous Lover
Her hands whilst they're my food bestowing
A thousand graces will be showing
And smiles enliven every feature
Whilst I engage her youthful nature
To mind my little tricks and fancies
My active play and circling dances
And if by a genteel behaviour
'Tis but my lot to gain her favour
To her my life shall be devoted
And I as her first captive noted
Shall fill a mighty place in story
And share in that ambitious glory

* Phillis: a common name for a maiden or 'nymph' in pastoral poetry.

To which so many hearts are growing
Where loss of freedom shall be owing
To her whose chain my value raises
And makes me merit all your praises.

(wr. before 1720, pub. 1988)

Elizabeth Singer Rowe
(ENGLAND, 1674–1737)

Parthenea, an Elegy

With Singing Angels hence she posts away,
As Lovely now and excellent as they:
For one short Moment Death's Grim Looks she bore,
But ne'r shall see his Ghastly Visage more.
Released from her dull Fetters; as the Light,
Active, and Pure, Parthenia takes her flight;
And finds, at last, the awful Secrecy,
How Spirits act, and what they do, and be.
But now she's swallow'd in a flood of Light,
And scarce endures the Splendour of the Sight:
Dear Shade, whom Heaven did so soon remove
From these Cold Regions to the Land of Love;
To endless Pleasures, and Eternal day;
How glittering now? How satisfy'd and gay
Art thou? methinks I do but half lament
The Lovely Saint from my Embraces rent:
Nor can to those fair Mansions cast my eyes,
To which she's fled, and not recall my sighs.
My grief for her were as unjust, as vain,
If from that Bliss 'twould hurry her again:
For tho' the Charming'st Friend on Earth I've lost,
Yet she the while may the advantage boast:

And should her pure unfetter'd Soul but deign
A careless glance on these dark coasts again,
'Twould Smile, as Conscious, where she left her Chain;
And smile again at the surprizing odds
Of her late dwelling, and those bright abodes;
Those bright abodes where now, securely blessed,
She Sings the Anthems of Eternal rest.

(1696)

To Cleone

From the bright realms, and happy fields above,
The seats of pleasure, and immortal love;
Where joys no more on airy chance depend,
All health to thee from those gay climes I send!
For thee my tender passion is the same,
Nor death itself has quench'd the noble flame;
For charms like thine for ever fix the mind,
And with eternal obligations bind.
And when kind fate shall my *Cleone* free
From the dull fetters of mortality,
I'll meet thy parting soul, and guide my fair
In triumph, thro' the lightsome fields of air;
'Till thou shalt gain the blissful seats and bow'rs,
And shining plains deck'd with unfading flow'rs.
There nobler heights our friendship shall improve,
For flames, like ours, bright spirits feel above,
And tune their golden harps to the soft notes of love.
The sacred subject swells each heav'nly breast,
And in their looks its transports are expressed.

(pub. 1739)

Anonymous

Cloe to Artimesa

While vulgar souls their vulgar love pursue,
And in the common way themselves undo;
Impairing health and fame, and risking life,
To be a mistress or, what's worse, a wife:
We, whom a nicer* taste has raised above
The dangerous follies of such slavish love,
Despise the sex,† and in our selves we find
Pleasures for their gross senses too refined.
Let brutish men, made by our weakness vain,
Boast of the easy conquest they obtain;
Let the poor loving wretch do all she can,
And *all* won't please th' ungrateful tyrant, Man;
We'll scorn the monster and his mistress too,
And show the world what women ought to do.

(1720)

---

* nicer: more subtle or fastidious.
† the sex: the other sex, men.

Elizabeth Thomas
(ENGLAND, 1675–1731)

To Clemena

Clemena, if you are indeed
The Friend you have professed,
Your Kindness now exert with Speed,
And give me back my *Rest*.
Late in our gloomy Shade I sat,
Retir'd from all domestic Care,
And tho' as calm as was th' Air,
Yet soon disturb'd like that.
For while I grasp'd my precious Store,
And read your last kind Letters o'er,
The gay *Melinda* pass'd along,
And cried, Oh where is Friendship gone!
What makes *Eliza* look so down,
When fair *Clemena's* come to Town?
Indeed, methinks she's much your Friend,
So near, and neither come nor send.
Nay, prithee do not turn away,
'Ere you have heard what I can say.
Alas, I much lament your Case,
For haughty *Gallia* takes your Place;
Her *Clemena* gives her Heart,
And leaves you not the smallest Part.

Judge with what Grief I was possessed,
How Love and Anger tore my Breast:
Is this, said I, her kind Return,
For all my tender Cares?
Did I for this my Life despise,
And venture it for hers?

Did I for this, such Frowns endure,
Such Hatred to my self procure?
And can she with her Vows Expence,
Now make this cruel Recompence?
But when this Storm was somewhat laid,
I fancied that I was betray'd;
For looking round the Nymph was gone,
And mock'd from far my piteous Moan:
'Twas then, you came into my Mind,
So nobly faithful, and so kind:
That I can hardly think it true,
But wait to be resolv'd by you.

(1722)

Mary Masters

(ENGLAND, *c.* 1694–1771)

To the Same; Enquiring Why I Wept

You fix a Dagger in my Heart,
You wound me in the tend'rest Part,
And then enquire the Reason of my Smart.

Alas! you talk of Death and Woe
That you must quickly undergo;
Yet ask the Cause whence all my Sorrows flow.

Ah! do you think my Love so small,
That I could part with Thee, my all,
Yet not permit one friendly Tear to fall?

Tell me, my dear Olinda, why
You question my Fidelity,
Methinks with Thee I cou'd ev'n wish to die.

(1733)

Elizabeth Teft

(ENGLAND, 1723–after 1747)

On a Friend's taking a Journey

Be all serene, thou dull inclement Sky;
Be hush, ye Winds; Avenues all, be dry.
Nor you, ye Roads, your rugged Garments wear;
Let Nature in her blooming Spring appear;
Be swift, ye Steeds; smoothly, ye Wheels, turn round,
And each Material in true Order found.
Fair Orb of Warmth, thy gentle Influence shed,
And sporting Zephyrs,* play around her Head;
Thou sweet Composer, be her Mind's fair Guest,
And cheerful Peace inhabit in her Breast;
With Notes harmonious charm her, O ye Train
Of Feather'd Choristers, that skim the Plain.
Time, dress her Hours with most sublime Delight,
With Joy the Day, with peaceful Sleep the Night.
The Journey at a Period, may she find
All Things concurring better than design'd.
Success and lasting Plenty crown her State,
Long Life, Joy-giving Health her Person wait.
Blessed in each Wish, return, return, my Friend,
And do not long our meeting Joy suspend.

(1747)

* Zephyrs: gentle winds, named for Zephyrus, the west wind in classical
mythology.

Charlotte MacCarthy

(IRELAND AND ENGLAND, mid eighteenth century)

Contentment, to a Friend

This small Repast, with her I love,
By her dear Hand thus neatly dress'd,
To me is more than if great *Jove*
Had bid me to an heavenly Feast.

When e'er she fills the little Cup
(Tho' from the Spring she brings the Treat)
With eager Joy I drink it up,
And Nectar ne'er was half so sweet.

The Trencher* which she laid herself,
Tho' plain, and homely to behold,
Is brighter than the Miser's Pelf,†
When form'd in Plates of shining Gold.

So where we love, the meanest Cell,
Is Peace, is Pleasure's rich Retreat;
Whilst gilded Courts, where Monarchs dwell,
Are Dungeons black, with those we hate.

(1745)

* trencher: platter.
† pelf: riches.

To the Same

Tell me, ye Registers of Fate,
Why thus my Soul with *Chloe* moves;
Why I abhor whom she must hate,
Or why I love whom *Chloe* loves.

Why when she frowns, my every Joy,
To dark Oblivion sinks away;
Or why her Smiles my Cares destroy,
And adds new Sunshine to my Day.

Were she (bright Nymph) some Shepherd Youth,
Then had I thought the little Loves
Had bid me quit romantic Truth,
And only dote whilst Beauty moves,

Said Fortune most completes our Bliss,
And Love with that flies swift away;
That cold's the Touch, the faint's the Kiss,
When Wealth and Beauty both decay.

But this is something more divine,
For tho' my *Chloe*'s Charms shou'd fade,
Her Beauty still to me wou'd shine,
Still I'd adore the heavenly Maid.

Tho' Fortune shunn'd her every Hour,
More dear to me wou'd *Chloe* prove,
Than if the Gods a golden Shower
Had sent to recompense my Love.

'Tis Friendship, noblest of the Mind,
'Tis that, that can this Difference make;
The Links of that in Heaven are join'd,
Which Time, or Fortune, ne'er can break.

(1745)

Susanna Highmore Duncombe

(ENGLAND, 1725–1812)

To Aspasia

Wisdom, Aspasia, by thy gentle muse,
   Warns me to shun the dang'rous paths of Love,
And rather those of sober Friendship choose,
   With cheerful Liberty in Dian's* grove.

Yet, led by Fancy through deceitful ground,
   Oft have I friendship sought, but sought in vain;
Unfaithful friends with myrtle wreaths I crown'd,
   Unpleasing subjects of my plaintive strain.

In youthful innocence, a school-day friend
   First gain'd my sister-vows; unhappy maid!
How did I wipe thy tears, thy griefs attend,
   And how was all my tenderness repaid!

No sooner Grandeur, Love, and Fortune smiled,
   Than base Ingratitude thy heart betrays,
That friend forgot, who all thy woes beguiled,
   Lost in the sun-shine of thy prosperous days.

Save me, kind Heav'n, from smiling Fortune's power!
   And may my wishes never meet success,
If e'er I can forget one single hour,
   The friend who gave me comfort in distress.

Yet Friendship's influence I again implored,
   To heal the wounds by Disappointment made;
Friendship my soul to balmy peace restored,
   And sent a gentle virgin to my aid.

* Dian: Diana, goddess of the forest, the hunt and maidens.

Soft, modest, pensive, melancholy Fair,
    She seem'd to Love and pining Grief a prey;
I saw her fading cheek, and feared Despair
    Fed on her heart and stole her life away.

But ah! how chang'd my friend! how vain my fears!
    Not death, but Hymen* stole her from my heart;
Another love dispell'd her sighs and tears,
    And Fame was left the secret to impart.

Not twice the changing moon her course had run,
    Since first the pleasing youth was seen and loved,
The Fair in secret haste he woo'd and won,
    No friend consulted, for no friend approved.

Suspense not long my anxious bosom pain'd,
    My friend arrived, I clasp'd her to my breast,
I wept, I smiled, alternate passions reign'd,
    Till she the sad unwelcome tale confess'd.

Lost to her brother, country, and to me,
    A stranger wafts her to a foreign shore,
She travels mountains and defies the sea,
    Nor thinks of Albion† or of Stella more.

Sure nature in her weakest, softest mould,
    Form'd my unhappy heart, False Friendship's prey!
Another story yet remains untold,
    Which fond Compassion bids me not display;

The lovely sister of a faithless friend,
    Weeping entreats me spare the recent tale;
Her sighs I hear, her wishes I attend,
    And o'er her sister's failings draw the veil.

* Hymen: the god of marriage.
† Albion: Great Britain.

This my success in search of Friendship's grove,
    Where Liberty and Peace I hoped to find,
And soften'd thus with grief, deceitful Love,
    In Friendship's borrow'd garb, attack'd my mind.

No passion raging like the roaring main,
    But calm and gentle as a summer sea,
Meek Modesty and Virtue in his train,
    What Friendship ought, true Love appear'd to be.

But soon was chang'd, alas! the pleasing scene,
    Soon threat'ning Storms my timid heart alarm'd;
And Love no more appear'd with brow serene,
    But cloth'd in terrors, and with dangers arm'd.

From these enchanted bow'rs my steps I turn,
    And seek from Prudence, safety and repose;
Her rigid lessons I resolve to learn,
    And gain that bliss which self-approof bestows.

Thus, dear Aspasia, my unhappy fate,
    My heart's first darling schemes all blasted, see;
Yet now my bosom glows with hope elate,
    Fair Friendship's blessings still to find with thee

By thee conducted to the realms of Peace,
    No more in plaintive strains the muse shall sing.
Henceforth with hymns of praise, and grateful bliss,
    The groves shall echo, and the valleys ring.

(wr. *c.* 1751, pub. 1775)

Charlotte Lennox

(USA AND ENGLAND, c. 1729–1804)

Ardelia to Flavia, an Epistle

Thou dearest Object of my fondest Love,
What Words can speak the Misery I prove?
Doom'd as I am by my relentless Fate,
To bear the worst of dreaded Ills, your Hate.
Lov'd tho' thou wert, in every Action just,
Have I not wrong'd thee by unkind Distrust?
Believ'd thee false, when Love and Truth were thine,
And all the tender joys of Friendship mine?
Wretch that I am, my fatal crime I know,
And merit all the Anger you can show.
Do hate me, loath me, drive me from your Breast,
That Seat of Softness, Innocence, and Rest!
Bid me my fatal Rashness ever mourn;
Fly my loath'd Sight, and curse me with your Scorn.
But oh! tho' Anger should each Grace transform,
And change to Roughness every smiling Charm:
Tho' those bright Eyes where Love and Sweetness shine,
Shou'd with the coldest Glances look on mine:
Tho' that harmonious, that enchanting Tongue,
Where all the Force of soft Persuasion hung,
Chide me in cruel Sounds, with Fury warm'd,
And wound the Ears it has so often charm'd:
Still wou'd I bear it all, with Patience bear,
And whisper to my Soul your Triumph there.
But sure, in Pity to my tender Pain,
Some Spark of Friendship in thy Breast remains:
To that I'll sue, the languid Flame to raise,
And wake the sleeping Passion to a Blaze:

Try every Art thy Anger to control,
And watch each yielding Moment in thy Soul;
Some tender Fit of Softness in thy Breast,
When Love's awake, and Anger charm'd to Rest.
For sure my *Flavia* cannot always prove
Deaf to the tender Prayers and Tears of Love.
Oh teach me, thou fair Softness, to atone
For all the Wrongs I've to thy Friendship done.
With thy own Sweetness thy just Rage disarm,
And learn me all thy well-known Power to charm.
Direct me how to make my Vows believ'd,
To move thy Pity, and thy Love retrieve.
Oh with returning Ardour ever bless
The Heart which you, and only you possess.

(1747)

Anna Seward*

(ENGLAND, 1742–1809)

Sonnet X

To Honora Sneyd

Honora, should that cruel time arrive
When 'gainst my truth thou should'st my errors poise,
Scorning remembrance of our vanish'd joys;
When for the love-warm looks, in which I live,
But cold respect must greet me, that shall give
No tender glance, no kind regretful sighs;
When thou shalt pass me with averted eyes,
Feigning thou see'st me not, to sting, and grieve,

* Seward: pronounced like 'seaward'.

And sicken my sad heart, I could not bear
Such dire eclipse of thy soul-cheering rays;
I could not learn my struggling heart to tear
From thy loved form, that thro' my memory strays;
Nor in the pale horizon of despair
Endure the wintry and the darken'd days.

(wr. 1773, pub. 1799)

Sonnet XXXI

To the Departing Spirit of an Alienated Friend

O, ever dear! thy precious, vital powers
Sink rapidly! – the long and dreary night
Brings scarce an hope that morn's returning light
Shall dawn for thee! – In such terrific* hours,
When yearning fondness eagerly devours
Each moment of protracted life, his flight
The rashly-chosen of thy heart has ta'en
Where dances, songs, and theatres invite.
Expiring Sweetness! with indignant pain
I see him in the scenes where laughing glide
Pleasure's light forms; – see his eyes gaily glow,
Regardless of thy life's fast ebbing tide;
I hear him, who should droop in silent woe,
Declaim on actors, and on taste decide!

(wr. 1780, pub. 1799)

* terrific: terrifying.

Elizabeth Hands

(ENGLAND, late eighteenth century)

An Epistle

My dear Maria, my long absent friend,
If you can spare one moment to attend,
The plaintive strains of your Belinda hear,
Who is your friend, and as yourself sincere.
Let love-sick nymphs their faithful shepherds prove,
Maria's friendship's more to me than love;
When you were here, I smil'd throughout the day,
No rustic shepherdess was half so gay;
But now, alas! I can no pleasure know,
The tedious hours of absence move so slow;
I secret mourn, not daring to complain,
Still seeking for relief, but seek in vain.
When I walk forth to take the morning air,
I quickly to some rising hill repair,
From whence I may survey your village spire,
Then sigh to you, and languish with desire.
At sultry noon retiring to the groves,
In search of you, my wand'ring fancy roves,
From shade to shade, pleas'd with the vain delight,
Imagination brings you to my sight;
Fatigu'd I sink into my painted chair,
And your ideal form attends me there.
My garden claims one solitary hour,
When sober ev'ning closes ev'ry flow'r;
The drooping lily my resemblance bears,
Each pensive bloom a shining dew-drop wears;
Such shining drops my closing eyes bedew,
While I am absent from the sight of you.

When on my couch reclin'd my eyes I close,
The God of Sleep refuses me repose;
I rise half dress'd, and wander to and fro
Along my room, or to my window go:
Enraptur'd I behold the moon shine clear,
While falling waters murmur in my ear;
My thoughts to you then in a moment fly,
The moon shines misty, and my raptures die.
Thus ev'ry scene a gloomy prospect wears,
And ev'ry object prompts Belinda's tears:
'Tis you, Maria, and 'tis only you,
That can the wonted face of things renew:
Come to my groves; command the birds to sing,
And o'er the meadows bid fresh daisies spring:
No! rather come and chase my gloom away,
That I may sing like birds, and look like daisies gay.

(1789)

Anne Grant

(SCOTLAND AND USA, 1755–1838)

The Nymph of the Fountain to Charlotte

Fair daughter of that fleeting race
    Who fade like Autumn's leafy store,
Welcome, my rocky haunts to trace,
    And all my secret cells explore.

Full many an oak, whose lofty head
    With sacred miseltoe was crown'd,
Since first I own'd that stony bed,
    Sunk dodder'd to its native ground.

And many a towering grove of pine,
   Whose gloom shut out the noon-day sun,
In shatter'd ruin lies supine,
   Since first my wat'ry course begun.

And many a toiling race of man
   Has joy'd in youth, and mourn'd in age,
Since first my pensive view began
   To trace their weary pilgrimage.

And many a nymph with sounding bow,
   Slow-rolling eyes, and heavy locks,
As young, as fair, as soft as thou,
   Has chas'd the deer o'er yonder rocks.

And when the sun's meridian heat
   With fervid splendour fir'd the heath,
Oft have they sought my cool retreat,
   With glowing breast and panting breath.

Yet, never did I pour my stream
   To bathe a breast more pure than thine,
Or visit eyes in whose mild beam
   So clear the gentler virtues shine.

When with light step thy naked feet
   Move quick my primrose banks along,
I bid my streams with murmur sweet
   Their liquid melody prolong.

When Echo to thy voice replies
   From yonder arch of rugged stone,
Well pleas'd I lift my humid eyes,
   As blue and languid as thy own:

When from yon hazel's pendant shade
 Sweet spring awakes the blackbird's strain,
Come to my bosom, gentle maid,
 And lave* thy streaming locks again.

Pluck from my brink the flow'ry store
 That blushing decks the infant year,
And to increase their beauty more,
 Deign round thy brow the wreath to wear.

And when the summer's ardent glow
 Shrinks every brook in yonder plain,
Come where my lucid waters flow,
 And bathe thy graceful form again.

Nor yet, when wint'ry tempests howl,
 To haunt my lonely margin cease,
Thro' life's dark storms the virtuous soul
 Finds Reason's steady light increase.

Hard ice, that crusts my current clear,
 Renews more pure my sparkling stream;
Thus may Affliction's hand severe
 Add lustre to the mental gem.

Where'er you rove, where'er you rest,
 May Peace your pensive steps attend,
And halcyon Innocence your breast
 From each contagious blast defend!

(1803)

---

* lave: wash.

Sarah Ponsonby

(IRELAND AND WALES, 1755–1831)

Song

By vulgar Eros long misled,
I call'd thee Tyrant, mighty Love!
With idle fear my fancy fled
Nor e'en thy pleasures wish'd to prove.

Condemn'd at length to wear thy chains,
Trembling I felt and ow'd thy might;
But soon I found my fears were vain,
Soon hugged my chain, and found it light.

(wr. 1789, pub. 1930)

Georgiana Spencer, Duchess of Devonshire

(ENGLAND, 1757–1806)

To Lady Elizabeth Foster, from Georgiana, Duchess of Devonshire, when she was apprehensive of losing her eyesight – 1796

The Life of the Roebuck was mine,
As I bounded o'er Valley and Lawn;
I watched the gay Twilight decline,
And worshipp'd the day-breaking Dawn.

I regret not the freedom of will,
Or sigh, as uncertain I tread;
I am freer and happier still,
When by thee, I am carefully led.

Ere my Sight I was doomed to resign,
My heart I surrendered to thee;
Not a Thought or an Action was mine,
But I saw as thou badst me to see.

Thy watchful affection I wait,
And hang with Delight on Thy voice;
And Dependence is softened by Fate,
Since Dependence on Thee is my Choice.

(wr. 1796, pub. 1890)

Eliza Cobbe, Lady Tuite
(IRELAND AND ENGLAND, 1764–1850)

To a Friend,
Fearful of being Forgotten in Absence

Time, while it Beauty's pow'r impairs,
Will only add to thine;
The di'mond, as its surface wears,
Does but the brighter shine.

Nor think regard, by Worth inspir'd,
E'en absence can subdue;
The sun, howe'er so long retir'd,
Still finds the dial true.

(1796)

Eliza Robertson

(ENGLAND, 1771–1805)

from A Poetical Epistle to an Absent Friend

O place us, dear Saviour! in some small retreat,
Let the banks, strew'd with daisies, afford us a seat;
Where the birds on the boughs do merrily sing,
And cuckoo proclaims the glad morning of spring.

Thy peace for our pillow – away from all noise,
Let us give and receive all friendship's true joys.
Where the soil it is healthy, and temp'rate air;
To add to our prospect, a little parterre:*

Where a lettuce and rose should be planted with taste,
And none of the group be left running to waste.
Instead of Italians,† the linnet and thrush
With harmony greet us, from ev'ry bush.

Our furniture clean, simple and plain,
Not anything gaudy, expensive or vain.
A shelf with good authors we surely would choose,
That, when serious or gay, might instruct and amuse.

No new-fashion'd novel, or gilded romance,
Should there have a place, if it travell'd from France.
Where my Charlotte could sleep on a pillow of down,
And, O! from Eliza, may she ne'er meet a frown.

May our table be spread with good wholesome cheer,
No kickshaws,‡ or lux'ry, shall ever be there.
Let not modern extravagance ever get root,
Our garden may yield a plate of good fruit.

---

*   parterre: flower-beds in a formal garden.
†   Italians: opera singers.
‡   kickshaws: fancy dish (from Fr. *quelquechose*).

A glass, too, of port, if health should require;
A shade when it's hot; when cold, a good fire.
To add to my comfort, may the Lord bless and lend
You, my dear Charlotte – compassionate friend!

(1801)

Margaretta Faugeres

(USA, 1771–1801)

Friendship

Friendship! I hate thy name – my rankled heart,
Forever wounded by thy treacherous hand,
Bleeding afresh defies the power of art,
Its pangs to soften, or extract the smart;
For who, ah who can draw the bitter dart
Implanted by a chosen, bosom friend?
Too long I harbour'd thee within my breast,
Thou base destroyer of my rest;
Too long thy galling yoke did bear:
For while I cherish'd thee with fostering care,
Thou didst thy pois'nous sting prepare,
And wrung the heart that fondly thee caressed.
But now adieu, thy reign is o'er,
For thee that heart no longer sighs;
And at thy voice shall joy no more
Suffuse this cheek, nor grace these eyes.
Thy ev'ry transport I'll forgo,
Thy sov'reignty disclaim;
And if no more thy sweets I know,
I know no more thy pain.
Tranquil my hours shall glide away,
No more a prey to poignant woes;

Content shall bless each rising day,
And charm each night with calm repose.
No more shall tears stray down my cheek,
Wak'd by thy sympathetic voice,
Nor griefs, too big for utterance, break
An injur'd heart that venerates thy ties;
Nor sighs all eloquent a language teach,
That mocks the idle power of speech.
Thus, once in anguish'd mind I wept and sung;
Warm from the heart th' unfeeling accents sprung;
For Perfidy's cold touch had chill'd
Each softer, gentler motion there,
And ev'ry painful chasm had fill'd
With weak mistrust and fretful care.
But vain I sought those scenes of bliss,
Which Fancy's flatt'ring pencil drew;
When the delights of smiling Peace
Each hour should brighten as it flew:
With Friendship ev'ry joy had fled,
With her each rapture took its flight;
Nor longer charm'd the branching shade,
Nor fragrant morn, nor spangled night.
In vain for me the songster swell'd its throat,
In vain the buds their moisten'd sweets disclose;
Nor cheer'd their glowing tints, nor sooth'd the note;
Alas! the selfish heart no pleasure knows.
'Ah, Hope!' sigh'd I, 'are these thy proffer'd joys?
Are these the hours of bliss that should be mine?
Few have I known since loos'd from Friendship's ties.'
Again my vows I offer'd at her shrine.
Sudden, as from *Castalia*'s favour'd spring,*
As sweet, as soft a tone I hear,

---

* Castalia's favour'd spring: Castaly is a fountain sacred to the Muses, the
waters of which inspire the drinker to write poetry.

As ever floated on mild Ev'ning's wing,
Or sooth'd pale Echo's ear.
Caught by the strain, each tear forgot to flow,
Each bitter rising murmur straight repressed;
When, with enchanting air and placid brow,
The lovely fair *Calista* stood confessed.
In feelings lost, tumultuously sweet,
Exultingly I own'd her gentle sway,
And blessed the heart whose sympathetic beat
Hail'd the young dawn of Friendship's rising day.

(1793)

Elizabeth Moody

(ENGLAND, *d.* 1814)

To a Lady, Who was a great Talker

If your friendship to take I must take too your clack,
That friendship, methinks, I could almost give back;
Yet for worlds would I not with your amity part,
Could you lock up your tongue when you open your heart.

(1798)

To a Friend,
Who gave the Author a Reading Glass

Still to my sight thy love doth rise
    To bless each state I pass!
The same I met with youthful eyes,
    I *see* through Age's *glass*.

(1798)

Dorothy Wordsworth

(ENGLAND, 1771–1855)

Irregular Verses

Ah Julia! ask a Christmas rhyme
Of *me* who in the golden time
Of careless, hopeful, happy youth
Ne'er strove to decorate the truth,
Contented to lay bare my heart
To one dear Friend, who had her part
In all the love and all the care
And every joy that harboured there.
– To her I told in simple prose
Each girlish vision, as it rose
Before an active busy brain
That needed neither spur nor rein,
That still enjoyed the present hour
Yet for the *future* raised a tower
Of bliss more exquisite and pure
Bliss that (so deemed we) should endure
Maxims of caution, prudent fears
Vexed not the projects of those years
Simplicity our steadfast theme,
No works of Art adorned our scheme. –
A cottage in a verdant dell,
A foaming stream, a crystal Well,
A garden stored with fruit and flowers
And sunny seats and shady bowers,
A file of hives for humming bees
Under a row of stately trees
And, sheltering all this faery ground,
A belt of hills must wrap it round,

Not stern or mountainous, or bare,
Nor lacking herbs to scent the air;
Nor ancient trees, nor scattered rocks,
And pastured by the blameless flocks
That print their green tracks to invite
Our wanderings to the topmost height.

Such was the spot I fondly framed
When life was new, and hope untamed:
There with my one dear Friend would dwell,
Nor wish for aught beyond the dell.
Alas! the cottage fled in air,
The streamlet never flowed:
– Yet did those visions pass away
So gently that they seemed to stay,
Though in our riper years we each pursued a different way.

– We parted, sorrowful; by duty led;
My Friend, ere long a happy Wife
Was seen with dignity to tread
The paths of usefulness, in active life;
And such her course through later days;
The same her honour and her praise;
As thou canst witness, thou dear Maid,
One of the Darlings of her care;
Thy *Mother* was that Friend who still repaid
Frank confidence with unshaken truth:
This was the glory of her youth,
A brighter gem than shines in prince's diadem.

You ask why in that jocund time
Why did I not in jingling rhyme
Display those pleasant guileless dreams
That furnished still exhaustless themes?
– I *reverenced* the Poet's skill,
And *might have* nursed a mounting Will

To imitate the tender Lays
Of them who sang in Nature's praise;
But bashfulness, a struggling shame
A fear that elder heads might blame
– Or something worse – a lurking pride
Whispering my playmates would deride
Stifled ambition, checked the aim
If e'er by chance 'the numbers* came'
– Nay even the mild maternal smile,
That oft-times would repress, beguile
The over-confidence of youth,
Even that dear smile, to own the truth,
Was dreaded by a fond self-love;
''Twill glance on me – and to reprove
Or,' (sorest wrong in childhood's school)
'Will *point* the sting of ridicule.'

And now, dear Girl, I hear you ask
Is this your lightsome, chearful task?
You tell us tales of forty years,
Of hopes extinct, of childish fears,
Why cast among us thoughts of sadness
When we are seeking mirth and gladness?
Nay, ill those words befit the Maid
Who pleaded for my Christmas rhyme
Mirthful she is; but placid – staid –
Her heart beats to no giddy chime
Though it with Chearfulness keeps time
For Chearfulness, a willing guest,
Finds ever in her tranquil breast
A fostering home, a welcome rest.
And well she knows that, casting *thought* away,
We lose the best part of each day;

* numbers: poetry.

That joys of youth remembered when our youth is past
Are joys that to the end of life will last;

And if this poor memorial strain,
Breathed from the depths of years gone by,
Should touch her Mother's heart with tender pain,
Or call a tear into her loving eye,
She will not check the tear or still the rising sigh.
– The happiest heart is given to sadness;
The saddest heart feels deepest gladness.

Thou dost not ask, thou dost not need
A verse from me; nor wilt thou heed
A greeting masked in laboured rhyme
From one whose heart has still kept time
With every pulse of thine

(wr. 1827, pub. 1987)

Mary Matilda Betham

(ENGLAND, 1776–1852)

In a Letter to A. R. C.
on Her Wishing to be Called Anna

Forgive me, if I wound your ear,
    By calling of you Nancy,
Which is the name of my sweet friend,
    The other's but her fancy.

Ah, dearest girl! how could your mind
    The strange distinction frame?
The whimsical, unjust caprice,
    Which robs you of your name.

Nancy agrees with what we see,
   A being wild and airy;
Gay as a nymph of Flora's train,
   Fantastic as a fairy.

But *Anna's* of a different kind,
   A melancholy maid;
Boasting a sentimental soul,
   In solemn pomp array'd.

Oh ne'er will I forsake the sound,
   So artless and so free!
Be what you will with all mankind,
   But *Nancy* still with me.

(1797)

Sydney Owenson, Lady Morgan

(IRELAND AND ENGLAND, 1776–1859)

Fragment III

To Mrs Lefanu

Oh why are not all those close ties which enfold
Each human connexion like those which unite us!
Why should interest* or pride, or feelings so cold,
Alone to sweet amity's bondage invite us?

Thou were just in that age when the soul's brightest ray
Illumines each mellowing charm of the face,
And the graces of youth still delightedly play
O'er each mind-beaming beauty which Time cannot chase.

---

* interest: self-seeking motives.

I was young, inexperienc'd, unknowing, unknown,
Wild, ardent, romantic, a stranger to thee;
But I'd heard worth, wit, genius, were all, all thine own;
And forgetting that thou wert a stranger to me

My heart overflowing, and new to each form
Of the world, I sought thee, nor fear'd to offend
By unconscious presumption: oh sure 'twas some charm
That thus led me to seek in a stranger, a friend!

Yes, yes, 'twas a charm of such magical force
As Reason herself never wish'd to repel,
For it drew its sweet magic from Sympathy's source,
And Reason herself bows to Sympathy's spell.

Yet fearful of failing and wishful of pleasing,
How timidly anxious thy notice I woo'd!
But oh! thy first warm glance each wild doubt appeasing,
With courage, with fondness, my faint heart endu'd.*

No never (till mem'ry by death shall be blighted)
Can our first touching interview fade from my mind,
When thou, all delighting, and I all delighted,
I, more than confiding; thou much more than kind.

Forgetful scarce germ'd was our friendship's young flower,
My heart o'er my lips unrestrain'd seem'd to rove,
Whilst thou sweetly veiling thy Mind's Brighter power,
Left me much to admire, yet still more to love.

Till warm'd by a kindness endearing, as dear,
A wild, artless song was respir'd for thee;
'Twas a national lay! and oh! when shall the tear
Which was shed o'er that song, be forgotten by me.

* endu'd: provided with.

And now since that sweet day some years have flown by,
And some golden hours of those years have been mine;
But each year as it fled never twisted one tie,
Round my heart, like that tie which first bound it to thine.

(1807)

Mary Russell Mitford

(ENGLAND, 1786–1855)

Written in a Blank-Paper Book
Given to the Author by a Friend

My little book, as o'er thy page so white,
    With half-closed eyes in idlest mood I lean,
    Whose is the form that rises still between
Thy page and me, – a vision of delight?
Look on those eyes by the bright soul made bright;
    Those curls, which who Antinous' bust* hath seen
    Hath loved; that shape which might beseem a queen;
That blush of purity; that smile of light.
    'Tis she! my little book dost thou not own†
Thy mistress? She it is, the only she!
    Dost thou not listen for the one sweet tone
Of her unrivalled voice? Dost thou not see
    Her look of love, for whose dear sake alone,
My little book, thou are so dear to me?

(1827)

---

* Antinous' bust: Antinous, favourite companion of the Roman Emperor
Hadrian, was considered a model of manly beauty.
† own: acknowledge.

Dorothea Primrose Campbell

(SCOTLAND AND ENGLAND, 1793–1863)

To Miss Sophia Headle

Say, dear Sophia! gentle friend,
    Wilt thou to Orkney's sea-beat strand
Again thy wand'ring footsteps bend,
    And leave fair England's happy land?

When o'er the murm'ring billows borne,
    As whisp'ring breezes waft you there,
Wilt thou with fond remembrance turn
    To her, that did thy pillow share?

When summer clothes each hill and dell
    Of Ronaldsha, with verdant sweets;
And Echo, from her sacred cell,
    The murmurs of the wave repeats;

As through our favourite haunts you stray,
    Will Mem'ry waken in thy mind,
And fancy by thy side portray
    The friend whom thou hast left behind?

And when the merry Lammas Fair
    Shall bid each country belle and beau
To Kirkwall's crowded street repair,
    Their wond'rous finery to show;

There, while the lively dance you join,
    Or list to music's melting strain –
Say, will one passing thought be mine
    Amid the gay and jocund train?

How oft, when wand'ring by the shore
   To catch the gentle ocean-breeze,
In many a sigh my soul I pour
   To thee, across the murm'ring seas!

I think upon thy tender cares,
   Sophia, with a tearful smile;
Pleasure and pain alternate shares
   The feelings of my breast the while.

'Twas thine, my sorrowing soul to sooth,
   When rack'd and torn by many a grief,
My rugged, slipp'ry path to smooth,
   And give my swelling heart relief.

Farewell, my friend! may peace be thine,
   Content, and health, and love, and joy;
And never may a grief like mine,
   Dear girl! thy bosom's peace alloy!

(1816)

Caroline Clive

(ENGLAND, 1801–73)

The Mosel

We passed a day on Mosel river, –
   Our day awaken'd with the sun,
It ended not till light was over,
   And then, alas! that it was done.

The early morn with dew was rife,
   The low light shadowing out the scene,
Noon, with intensity of life
   And evening bright with crimson sheen.

Through glorious shores it flow'd for ever,
   Reveal'd on our contented eyes,
It might have been that golden river,
   On both whose banks was Paradise.

I sat by thee, mine own dear friend,
   And thou and I were there alone,
That day at least, I did not fear
   That we should part ere day was done.

We saw those lovely things together,
   Which never will depart our mind,
We saw and felt that blessed river,
   Which now, alas! is far behind.

The liquid opal of the stream
   Dark with the light obliquely shed,
The reach far stretching to the beam,
   Then doubling back whence first it sped;

Successive villages that rose,
   Each with a spire address'd to God,
Quaint dwelling-places rear'd of those
   Who long since slept beneath the sod;

Groves bord'ring all the water-side,
   With pathways where the peasants stood,
And gath'ring into woods, whose pride
   Adorn'd the hills above the flood.

And where the porph'ry* rock threw out
   Before the sun its crimson sheet,
There vineyards spread their wealth about,
   Maturing in the noonday heat.

* porph'ry: porphyry, a hard reddish rock.

And then along some shelving shore
   The stream at times rushed swiftly past,
The boatman, resting on his oar,
   Let go our vessel light and fast.

And we among the sudden stir
   Of popping waves, were carried by,
And to each other smiled to mark
   The foam-flakes sparkle on the eye.

Oh joyous river! pleasant day!
   Not loud wert thou, but dear and bright;
And full of gladness, as the sky
   Is full of air, the day of light.

How joyful will it be to dwell
   On thee, if bright my future days,
But oh! if grief renew its spell,
   How sad will show thy former rays.

I pray thee, Time, reveal the way
   That lies before my steps for ever;
Shall I be glad or sorry, say,
   To think upon the Mosel river?

(1840)

Elizabeth Barrett Browning

(ENGLAND AND ITALY, 1806–61)

To George Sand

I.   A Desire

Thou large-brained woman and large-hearted man,
Self-called George Sand! whose soul, amid the lions
Of thy tumultuous senses, moans defiance,
And answers roar for roar, as spirits can!
I would some mild miraculous thunder ran
Above the applauded circus, in appliance
Of thine own nobler nature's strength and science,
Drawing two pinions, white as wings of swan,
From thy strong shoulders, to amaze the place
With holier light! that thou to woman's claim,
And man's, mightst join beside the angel's grace
Of a pure genius sanctified from blame –
Till child and maiden pressed to thine embrace,
To kiss upon thy lips a stainless fame.

II.   A Recognition

True genius, but true woman! dost deny
Thy woman's nature with a manly scorn,
And break away the gauds* and armlets worn
By weaker women in captivity?
Ah, vain denial! that revolted cry
Is sobbed in by a woman's voice forlorn! –
Thy woman's hair, my sister, all unshorn,
Floats back dishevelled strength in agony,

* gauds: ornaments.

Disproving thy man's name! and while before
The world thou burnest in a poet-fire,
We see thy woman-heart beat evermore
Through the large flame. Beat purer, heart, and higher,
Till God unsex thee on the heavenly shore,
Where unincarnate spirits purely aspire.

(1844)

Frances Kemble

(ENGLAND, USA, FRANCE AND ITALY, 1809–1903)

A Noonday Vision

I saw one whom I love more than my life
Stand on a perilous edge of slippery rock,
Under her feet the waters' furious strife,
And all around the thunder of their shock;
She stood and smiled, while terror held my breath,
Nor dared I speak, or move, or call, or cry,
Lest to wild measuring of the depth beneath,
From her small foothold she should turn her eye.
As in the tyrannous horror of a dream,
I could not look away, but stony, still,
Fastened my eyes on her, while she did seem
Like one that fears, but hath a steadfast will.
Around her, through green boughs, the sunlight flung
Its threads of glory like a golden net,
And all about the rock-wall where she clung,
The trembling crests of fern with stars were wet,
Bright beads of crystal on a rainbow strung,
Jewels of fire in drops of water set;

And while I gazed, a hand stretched forth to her,
Beckoned her on – and holding firm and fast
By this her unseen guide and monitor,
Behind the rocks out of my sight she passed,
And then the agony of all my fears
Broke forth from out my eyes in sudden tears,
And I fell weeping down upon the sod;
But in my soul I heard a voice that said
Be comforted – of what art thou afraid?
Not for the hand she holds be thou dismayed,
The hand that holds her is the hand of God.

(1866)

Parting

The golden hinges of the year have turned –
Spring, and the summer, and the harvest time
Have come, and gone; and on the threshold stands
The withered Winter, stretching forth his hands,
To take my rose from me; – which he will wear
On his bleak bosom, all the bitter months
While the earth and I remain disconsolate.
My rose! – with the soft vesture of her leaves,
Gathered all round the secrets of her heart,
In crimson fragrant folds, – within her bower
Of fair fresh green, guarded with maiden thorns.
Oh withered Winter! keep my blossom safe!
Thou shalt not kiss her with thy blue cold lips,
Nor pinch her in thy bony grip, – nor drop
More than one tiny sparkling diamond,
From thy cold carcanet,* upon her cheek:

* carcanet: a collar or necklace made of gold or jewels.

But lay soft snow fur round her – and above
Her precious head, make thy skies blue and clear,
And set her in the sun; – oh withered Winter!
Be tender of my rose, and harm her not.
Alas, my flower, farewell!

(1866)

Margaret Fuller

(USA AND ITALY, 1810–50)

To A. H. B.

On our meeting, on my return from N.Y. to Boston, August 1835

Brief was the meeting, – tear-stained, full of fears
    For future days, and sad thoughts of the past, –
    Thou, seeing thy horizon overcast,
Timid, didst shrink from the dark-coming years;
And I, (though less ill in mine appears,)
    Was haunted by a secret dread of soul,
    That Fate had something written in her scroll
Which soon must ope again the fount of tears,
    Oh could we on the waves have lingered then,
Or in that bark, together borne away,
    Have sought some isle far from the haunts of men,
Ills left behind which cloud the social day,
    What grief I had escaped; yet left untried
    That holy faith by which, now fortified,
    I feel a peace to happiness allied, –
And thou, although for thee my loving heart
Would gladly some Elysium* set apart,

* Elysium: a place of perfect happiness, literally the home of the blessed after death.

From treachery's pestilence, and passion's strife,
Where thou might'st lead a pure untroubled life,
Sustained and fostered by hearts like thy own,
The conflicts which thy friend must brave, unknown, –
Yet I feel deeply, that it may be best
For thee as me, that fire the gold should test,
And that in God's good time we shall know perfect rest!

(wr. 1836, pub. 1992)

Frances Osgood

(USA AND ENGLAND, 1811–50)

The Garden of Friendship

They say I am robbing myself,
    But they know not how sweet is my gain,
For I'm weeding my garden of Friendship,
    Till only its flowers remain.

They say if I weed from it all
    That are worldly, ignoble, untrue,
I shall save not a leaf for my heart;
    But they shake not my faith in the few.

I waste not the pure dew of Feeling,
    I waste not the warm light of Love
On worthless intruders, upstealing
    To poison the beauty above.

Too pure is the place, and too holy,
    For Falsehood and Sin to profane;
And I heed not how few or how lowly
    The blooms that unsullied remain.

Though lone and apart in their sweetness,
  Those heart-cherish'd blossoms may be,
While they smile in the sunlight of Truth,
  They suffice to affection and me.

And you, in your delicate bloom, love,
  Pure, tender, and graceful and true,
Shall be the queen-rose of my garden,
  And live on Love's sunshine and dew.

No parasite plant shall be nourish'd,
  My bower's sunny beauty to stain,
For I'll weed the fair garden of Friendship
  Till only its flowers remain.

(1850)

Isa Blagden

(ITALY, *c.* 1816–73)

Alice

In her golden chamber –
  Golden with the sun –
Where the roses clamber
  Breathless, one by one;

(O'er her casement creeping
  With their lavish grace,
Through her lattice peeping
  At her happy face,)

Sitteth fairest Alice
  Bending calmly there;
Roses, bear no malice,
  Ye are not so fair.

Bending o'er her missal,
  Alice sitteth there;
Shamrock, rose and thistle,
  Carved in jewels rare,

Clasp the velvet cover,
  With a rare device;
Scrolls are blazoned over
  Gold and azure dyes.

Argent* angels flying,
  Peacock's eyes and wings,
Martyrs bravely dying,
  Quaint and lovely things.

Rubies red, and glowing
  Pearls and emerald sheaves –
Sapphire rivers flowing,
  Glitter through the leaves.

I, a page, a servant,
  Alice as a queen
At my love so fervent
  Smiles, with pride serene.

All my love, my passion –
  All myself I give,
True to ancient fashion,
  Loving while I live.

Claiming nought from Alice,
  Knowing love is vain;
Wine poured from a chalice
  Flows not back again.

* argent: silver.

True love is a treasure
  Sacred and divine;
Without stint or measure
  Cast upon a shrine.

Alice is an altar
  Flaming with my love,
Where my prayers I falter
  As to heaven above.

Kneeling low before her,
  Every pulse and breath
Asks but to adore her,
  Faithful unto death.

(1873)

Emily Brontë

(ENGLAND, 1818–48)

Love and Friendship

Love is like the wild rose briar,
Friendship, like the holly tree
The holly is dark when the rose briar blooms,
But which will bloom most constantly?

The wild rosebriar is sweet in spring,
Its summer blossoms scent the air
Yet wait till winter comes again
And who will call the wild-briar fair

Then scorn the silly rose-wreath now
And deck thee with the holly's sheen
That when December blights thy brow
He still may leave thy garland green –

(pub. 1850)

Alice Cary

(USA, 1820–71)

The Window Just Over the Street

I sit in my sorrow a-weary, alone;
  I have nothing sweet to hope or remember,
For the spring o' the year and of life has flown;
  'Tis the wildest night o' the wild December,
  And dark in my spirit and dark in my chamber.

I sit and list to the steps in the street,
  Going and coming, and coming and going,
And the winds at my shutter they blow and beat;
  'Tis the middle of night and the clouds are snowing;
  And the winds are bitterly beating and blowing.

I list to the steps as they come and go,
  And list to the winds that are beating and blowing,
And my heart sinks down so low, so low;
  No step is stayed from me by the snowing,
  Nor stayed by the wind so bitterly blowing.

I think of the ships that are out at sea,
  Of the wheels in th' cold, black waters turning;
Not one of the ships bearest news to me,
  And my heart is sick, and my heart is yearning,
  As I think of the wheels in the black waters turning.

Of the mother I think, by her sick baby's bed,
  Away in her cabin as lonesome and dreary,
And little and low as the flax-breaker's shed;
  Of her patience so sweet, and her silence so weary,
  With cries of the hungry wolf hid in the prairie.

I think of all things in the world that are sad;
   Of children in homesick and comfortless places;
Of prisons, of dungeons, of men that are mad;
    Of wicked, unwomanly light in the faces
    Of women that fortune has wronged with disgraces.

I think of a dear little sun-lighted head,
   That came where no hand of us all could deliver;
And crazed with the cruelest pain went to bed
    Where the sheets were the foam-fretted waves of the river;
    Poor darling! may God in his mercy forgive her.

The footsteps grow faint and more faint in the snow;
   I put back the curtain in very despairing;
The masts creak and groan as th' winds come and go;
    And the light in the light-house all weirdly is flaring;
    But what glory is this, in the gloom of despairing!

I see at the window just over the street,
   A maid in the lamplight her love-letter reading.
Her red mouth is smiling, her news is so sweet;
    And the heart in my bosom is cured of its bleeding,
    As I look on the maiden her love-letter reading.

She has finished the letter, and folding it, kisses,
   And hides it – a secret too sacred to know;
And now in the hearth-light she softly undresses:
    A vision of grace in the roseate glow,
    I see her unbinding the braids of her tresses.

And now as she stoops to the ribbon that fastens
   Her slipper, they tumble o'er shoulder and face;
And now, as she patters in bare feet, she hastens
    To gather them up in a fillet of lace;
    And now she is gone, but in fancy I trace

The lavendered linen updrawn, the round arm
　　Half sunk in the counterpane's broidered roses,
Revealing the exquisite outline of form;
　　A willowy wonder of grace that reposes
　　Beneath the white counterpane, fleecy with roses.

I see the small hand lying over the heart,
　　Where the passionate dreams are so sweet in their sally;
The fair little fingers they tremble and part,
　　As part to th' warm waves the leaves of the lily,
　　And they play with her hand like the waves with the lily.

In white fleecy flowers, the queen o' the flowers!
　　What to her is the world with its bad, bitter weather?
Wide she opens her arms – ah, her world is not ours!
　　And now she has closed them and clasped them together –
　　What to her is our world, with its clouds and rough weather?

Hark! midnight! the winds and the snows blow and beat;
　　I drop down the curtain and say to my sorrow,
Thank God for the window just over the street;
　　Thank God there is always a light whence to borrow
　　When darkness is darkest, and sorrow most sorrow.

(wr. before 1871, pub. 1876)

Dora Greenwell

(ENGLAND, 1821–82)

To Elizabeth Barrett Browning, in 1851

I lose myself within thy mind – from room
   To goodly room thou leadest me, and still
   Dost show me of thy glory more, until
My soul, like Sheba's Queen,* faints, overcome,
And all my spirit dies within me, numb,
   Sucked in by thine, a larger star, at will;
   And hasting like thy bee, my hive to fill,
I 'swoon for very joy' amid thy bloom;
Till – not like that poor bird (as poets feign)
   That tried against the Lutanist's her skill,
   Crowding her thick precipitate notes, until
Her weak heart break above the contest vain –
   Did not thy strength a nobler thought instil,
I feel as if I ne'er could sing again!

(1867)

To Elizabeth Barrett Browning, in 1861

I praised thee not while living; what to thee
   Was praise of mine? I mourned thee not when dead;
   I only loved thee, – love thee! oh thou fled
Fair spirit, free at last where all are free,

---

* Sheba's Queen: in the Old Testament, when King Solomon answers all
the questions put to him by the Queen of Sheba, she becomes breathless
and acknowledges the truth of his god Yahweh; see 1 Kings 10:1–13; 2 Chr.
9:1–12.

I only love thee, bless thee, that to me
   For ever thou hast made the rose more red,
   More sweet each word by olden singers said
In sadness, or by children in their glee;
   Once, only once in life I heard thee speak,
   Once, only once I kissed thee on the cheek,
And met thy kiss and blessing; scarce I knew
Thy smile, I only loved thee, only grew,
   Through wealth, through strength of thine, less poor, less
     weak;
   Oh, what hath death with souls like thine to do?

(1867)

Reconciliation

Our waking hours write bitter things
   Against us on Life's wall;
But Sleep her small soft finger brings,
   And draws it through them all.
Oh! sweet her kiss on tired eyes,
   More sweet to make amends
Her child-kiss on the soul that lies,
   And sayeth, 'Come, be friends!'
One is there I have loved so long
   And deep, I know not when
I loved her not with Love too strong
   To change its *now* to *then*;
But Love had been with Love at war,
   And bitter words had been,
And silence bitterer by far
   Had come our souls between;

But now she came to me in sleep,
  Her eyes were on my soul:
Kind eyes! they said, 'And didst *thou* weep
  And *I* did not console?
Look up, and be no longer sad!'
  She called me by my name:
Our spirits rushed together, glad
  And swift as flame to flame;
And all the sweetness from my life
  Crushed out, and all the bloom
That wasted through those years of strife,
  And faded on their gloom,
Came back together; as of old
  She clasped me, then I knew
And spoke not, stirred not, fold by fold
  Our hearts together grew:
Then thought I – as in whisper soft,
  'We two have died, and this
Is joy that saints have told us of, –
  The meeting and the kiss.'
Such bliss, forgiving and forgiven,
  Ran through me while I slept,
To find the ties that Earth had riven
  Above were sacred kept;
And yet I knew it was not Heaven –
  Because I wept!

(1861)

Bessie Rayner Parkes

(ENGLAND AND FRANCE, 1829–1925)

Dream Fears

We met when time to both was young,
And even'd by our love it grew,
All scatter'd music which I sung
Was gather'd up and given by you.
Too mighty seems the golden spell
To bind it round with flowers of speech,
But high as heaven, or deep as hell,
I swear unbroken it shall reach.

If I should lose, – I cannot say
The thing, for light and thought and hope
Are so knit up in you, my way
So well companion'd in your scope,
That, if I try the words to speak
Which picture me without you here,
The shuddering thrills which o'er me break
Say, wordless, if your thought is dear.

If I should lose, – my dream flows on,
With the dark yearning in my eyes
Of one who thinks he sees the sun
Sink blackly thro' dissolving skies.
Oft as this dream sweeps over me,
Sore troubled in your eyes I look,
The phantom of my fear you see,
That is the gaze you cannot brook.

'If I lose you,' – I brave the word,
I will repeat it day by day;
Who boldly grasps a naked sword
Perchance can fling the blade away.
Oh give me back my causeless trust,
My hope that never knew a fear, –
Fate, if thou strike me into dust,
Let me not know when thou art near!

'If I lose you,' – if I should see
Your dearest face quite pale and cold,
And death's dark shadow silently
Even the lingering smile enfold,
Straight comb'd beside your pulseless heart,
Unbraided lie chill shining hair,
And flickering sunbeams glow and start,
With no caress responsive there.

And I, whose voice is often mute
When love wells up within my soul,
Dared all my mocking hope refute,
Retreating on a dumb control, –
I do not know, – I cannot paint
In dreams what such a loss would be;
But if it come, and my soul faint,
Dear God in Heaven, be strong for me –
Be strong for me!

(1854)

Christina Rossetti

(ENGLAND, 1830–94)

Gone Before

She was most like a rose, when it flushes rarest;
She was most like a lily, when it blows fairest;
She was most like a violet, sweetest on the bank:
Now she's only like the snow cold and blank
   After the sun sank.

She left us in the early days, she would not linger
For orange blossoms in her hair, or ring on finger:
Did she deem windy grass more good than these?
Now the turf that's between us and the hedging trees
   Might as well be seas.

I had trained a branch she shelters not under,
I had reared a flower she snapped asunder:
In the bush and on the stately bough
Birds sing; she who watched them track the plough
   Cannot hear them now.

Every bird has a nest hidden somewhere
For itself and its mate and joys that come there,
Tho' it soar to the clouds, finding there its rest:
You sang in the height, but no more with eager breast
   Stoop to your own nest.

If I could win you back from heaven-gate lofty,
Perhaps you would but grieve returning softly:
Surely they would miss you in the blessed throng,
Miss your sweet voice in their sweetest song,
   Reckon time too long.

Earth is not good enough for you, my sweet, my sweetest;
Life on earth seemed long to you tho' to me fleetest.
I would not wish you back if a wish would do:
Only love I long for heaven with you
   Heart-pierced thro' and thro'.

(wr. 1856, pub. before 1896)

Echo

Come to me in the silence of the night;
   Come in the speaking silence of a dream;
Come with soft rounded cheeks and eyes as bright
   As sunlight on a stream;
     Come back in tears,
O memory, hope, love of finished years.

Oh dream how sweet, too sweet, too bitter sweet
   Whose wakening should have been in Paradise,
Where souls brimfull of love abide and meet;
   Where thirsting longing eyes
     Watch the slow door
That opening, letting in, lets out no more.

Yet come to me in dreams, that I may live
   My very life again tho' cold in death:
Come back to me in dreams, that I may give
   Pulse for pulse, breath for breath:
     Speak low, lean low,
As long ago, my love, how long ago.

(wr. 1854, pub. 1862)

Emily Dickinson
(USA, 1830–86)

'Baffled for just a day or two'

Baffled for just a day or two –
Embarrassed – not afraid –
Encounter in my garden
An unexpected Maid.

She beckons, and the woods start –
She nods, and all begin –
Surely, such a country
I was never in!

(wr. *c.* 1858, pub. 1945)

'Her breast is fit for pearls'

Her breast is fit for pearls,
But I was not a 'Diver' –
Her brow is fit for thrones
But I have not a crest.
Her heart is fit for *home* –
I – a Sparrow – build there
Sweet of twigs and twine
My perennial nest.

(wr. *c.* 1859, pub. 1894)

'Wild Nights – Wild Nights!'

Wild Nights – Wild Nights!
Were I with thee
Wild Nights should be
Our luxury!

Futile – the Winds –
To a Heart in port –
Done with the Compass –
Done with the Chart!

Rowing in Eden –
Ah, the Sea!
Might I but moor – Tonight –
In Thee!

(wr. *c.* 1861, pub. 1891)

'"Heaven" – is what I cannot reach!'

'Heaven' – is what I cannot reach!
The Apple on the Tree –
Provided it do hopeless – hang –
That – 'Heaven' is – to Me!

The Color, on the Cruising Cloud –
The interdicted Land –
Behind the Hill – the House behind –
There – Paradise – is found!

Her teasing Purples – Afternoons –
The credulous – decoy –
Enamored – of the Conjuror –
That spurned us – Yesterday!

(wr. *c.* 1861, pub. 1896)

'I showed her Heights she never saw'

I showed her Heights she never saw –
'Would'st Climb,' I said?
She said – 'Not so' –
'With *me* – ' I said – With me?
I showed her Secrets – Morning's Nest –
The Rope the Nights were put across –
And *now* – 'Would'st have me for a Guest?'
She could not find her Yes –
And then, I brake my life – And Lo,
A Light, for her, did solemn glow,
The larger, as her face withdrew –
And *could* she, further, 'No'?

(wr. *c.* 1862, pub. 1914)

'Her face was in a bed of hair'

Her face was in a bed of hair,
Like flowers in a plot –
Her hand was whiter than the sperm*
That feeds the sacred light.
Her tongue more tender than the tune
That totters in the leaves –
Who hears may be incredulous,
Who witnesses, believes.

(pub. 1945)

---

* sperm: spermaceti, a white wax from the sperm whale used to make the best candles.

Helen Hunt Jackson

(USA, 1830–85)

Friends

To A. E. P.

We rode a day, from east, from west,
To meet. A year had done its best,
By absence, and by loss of speech,
To put beyond the other's reach
Each heart and life; but, drawing nigh,
'Ah! It is you!' 'Yes, it is I!'
We said; and love had been blasphemed
And slain in each had either deemed
Need of more words, or joy more plain
When eyes had looked in eyes again:
Ah friendship, stronger in thy might
Than time and space, as faith than sight!
Rich festival with thy red wine
My friend and I will keep in courts divine!

(pub. 1892)

Her Eyes

That they are brown, no man will dare to say
He knows. And yet I think that no man's look
Ever those depths of light and shade forsook,
Until their gentle pain warned him away.
Of all sweet things I know but one which may
Be likened to her eyes.
                            When, in deep nook
Of some green field, the water of a brook
Makes lingering, whirling eddy in its way,

Round soft drowned leaves; and in a flash of sun
They turn to gold, until the ripples run
Now brown, now yellow, changing as by some
Swift spell.
                    I know not with what body come
The saints. But this I know, my Paradise
Will mean the resurrection of her eyes.

(pub. 1892)

Annie Fields

(USA, 1834–1915)

Ephemeron*

'Behold,' she said, 'a falling star!'
    I followed where her vision led,
And saw no meteor near nor far;
    So swiftly sank the lustre, dead.

In silvery moonlight stood she there,
    Whiter than silver gleamed her hand,
And gleaming shone her yellow hair,
    While dusky shadows filled the land.

She seemed a slender flickering shape,
    Framed in the blackness of the porch.
How should a child of night escape!
    A foolish moth that loved the torch!

Out of my dusk I came to her:
    Voices were stilled, anear, afar;
I stood there lost, her worshipper;
    What eye beheld that falling star?

(1888)

---

* Ephemeron: an insect which, when it develops wings, lives for only a day.

To —, Sleeping

Belovëd, when I saw thee sleeping there,
And watched the tender curving of thy mouth,
The cheek, our home of kisses, the soft hair,
And over all a languor of the south;
And marked thy house of thought, thy forehead, where
All trouble of the earth was then at rest;
And thy dear eyes, a blessing to the blest,
Their ivory gates closed on this world of care, –

Then, then I prayed that never wrong of mine,
That never pain which haunts these earth-built bowers,
If I could hinder, or could aught relieve,
Should ever more make sad this heart of thine;
And yet, dear love, how oft thou leav'st thy flowers,
Here in the rain to walk with me and grieve!

(1895)

Adah Isaacs Menken

(USA, *c.* 1839–68)

Answer Me

In from the night.
The storm is lifting his black arms up to the sky.
Friend of my heart, who so gently marks out the life-track for
        me, draw near to-night;
Forget the wailing of the low-voiced wind:
Shut out the moanings of the freezing, and the starving, and
        the dying, and bend your head low to me:
Clasp my cold, cold hands in yours;
Think of me tenderly and lovingly:

Look down into my eyes the while I question you, and if you
        love me, answer me –
    Oh, answer me!

Is there not a gleam of Peace on all this tiresome earth?
Does not one oasis cheer all this desert-world?
When will all this toil and pain bring me the blessing?
Must I ever plead for help to do the work before me set?
Must I ever stumble and faint by the dark wayside?
Oh the dark, lonely wayside, with its dim-sheeted ghosts
        peering up through their shallow graves!
Must I ever tremble and pale at the great Beyond?
Must I find Rest only in your bosom, as now I do?
    Answer me –
    Oh, answer me!

Speak to me tenderly.
Think of me lovingly.
Let your soft hands smooth back my hair.
Take my cold, tear-stained face up to yours.
Let my lonely life creep into your warm bosom, knowing no
        other rest but this.
Let me question you, while sweet Faith and Trust are folding
        their white robes around me.
Thus am I purified, even to your love, that came like John the
        Baptist in the Wilderness of Sin.
You read the starry heavens, and lead me forth.
But tell me if, in this world's Judea, there comes never quiet
        when once the heart awakes?
Why must it ever hush Love back?
Must it only labor, strive, and ache?
Has it no reward but this?
Has it no inheritance but to bear – and break?
    Answer me –
    Oh, answer me!

The Storm struggles with the Darkness.

Folded away in your arms, how little do I heed their battle!

The trees clash in vain their naked swords against the door.

I go not forth while the low murmur of your voice is drifting
all else back to silence.

The darkness presses his black forehead close to the window
pane, and beckons me without.

Love holds a lamp in this little room that hath power to blot
back Fear.

But will the lamp ever starve for oil?

Will its blood-red flame ever grow faint and blue?

Will it uprear itself to a slender line of light?

Will it grow pallid and motionless?

Will it sink rayless to everlasting death?

    Answer me –

    Oh, answer me!

Look at these tear-drops.

See how they quiver and die on your open hands.

Fold these white garments close to my breast, while I
question you.

Would you have me think that from the warm shelter of your
heart I must go to the grave?

And when I am lying in my silent shroud, will you love me?

When I am buried down in the cold, wet earth, will you
grieve that you did not save me?

Will your tears reach my pale face through all the withered
leaves that will heap themselves upon my grave?

Will you repent that you loosened your arms to let me fall so
deep, and so far out of sight?

Will you come and tell me so, when the coffin has shut out
the storm?

    Answer me –

    Oh, answer Me!

(1868)

Mathilde Blind

(GERMANY, ENGLAND AND SWITZERLAND, 1841–96)

A Fantasy

I was an Arab,
  I loved my horse;
Swift as an arrow
  He swept the course.

Sweet as a lamb
  He came to hand;
He was the flower
  Of all the land.

Through lonely nights
  I rode afar;
God lit His lights –
  Star upon star.

God's in the desert;
  His breath the air:
Beautiful desert,
  Boundless and bare!

Free as the wild wind
  Light as a foal;
Ah, there is room there
  To stretch one's soul.

Far reached my thought.
  Scant were my needs:
A few bananas
  And lotus seeds.

Sparkling as water
  Cool in the shade,

Ibrahim's* daughter,
  Beautiful maid.

Out of thy Kulleh,
  Fairest and first,
Give me to drink
  Quencher of thirst.

I am athirst, girl;
  Parched with desire.
Love in my bosom
  Burns as a fire.

Green thy oasis,
  Waving with Palms;
Oh, be no niggard,
  Maid, with thy alms.

Kiss me with kisses,
  Buds of thy mouth,
Sweeter than Cassia,†
  Fresh from the South.

Bind me with tresses,
  Clasp with a curl;
And in caresses
  Stifle me, girl.

I was an Arab
  Ages ago!
Hence this home-sickness
  And all my woe.

(1895)

---

* Ibrahim: the Koranic version of Abraham.
† Cassia: a fragrant plant related to cinnamon.

Rosa Mulholland, Lady Gilbert

(NORTHERN IRELAND, IRELAND AND ENGLAND, 1841–1921)

A Stolen Visit

When you are wrapped in happy sleep,
  I walk about your house by night,
With many a wistful, stealthy peep
  At what I've loved by morning light.

Your head is on the pillow laid,
  My feet are where your footsteps were;
Your soul to other lands has strayed,
  My heart can hear you breathe and stir.

I seat me in your wonted chair,
  And ope your book a little space;
I touch the flowers that knew your care,
  The mirror that reflects your face.

I kiss the pen that spoke your thought,
  The spot whereon you knelt to pray,
The message with your wisdom fraught
  Writ down on paper yesterday,

The garment that you lately wore,
  The threshold that your step goes by,
The music that you fingered o'er,
  The picture that contents your eye.

Yet when you wake from happy sleep,
  And, busy here, and busy there,
You take your wonted morning peep
  At what is good and what is fair,

'She has been here,' you will not say,
   My prying face you will not find;
You'll think, 'She is a mile away,'
   My love hath left no mark behind.

(1886)

'Violet Fane'
(Mary Montgomerie Lamb Singleton Currie)

(ENGLAND, TURKEY AND ITALY, 1843–1905)

At Her Feet

As I lay at your feet the other day,
I opened a book with a gilded rim, –
   A silken 'Keepsake', wherein portrayed
   Simpering matron and star-eyed maid,
   With flowing ringlets and bosoms of snow,
   Peeped up from under the binding frayed,
   With sweet shy glances, their forms arrayed
   In the fanciful garments of long ago, –
And I toyed with its pages, and tried to skim
Some lordling's notion of poet's lay,
   And I thought, 'Fair ladies where are ye now,
Married, and buried, and hidden away,
Or grown, maybe, into grandams grim, –
   Where is the poet who rises and wakes
   His shuddering lyre for your faded sakes
Whose hairs are gray, and whose eyes are dim?
   So presently perish all things fair!' . . .
   Then, looking up, I saw you there,
   Under the shade of the chestnut bough,
   Your sun-hat tilted over your brow,

Almost hiding your rippling hair,
And with fair young figure, lithe and slim,
   Leaning back in your garden chair,
   Whilst your slender fingers, busily bare,
   Were knitting away at the second row
   Of something for somebody else to wear.
   And your spirit so far, *so far* from me,
   Who lay all the while so near your feet
   (Only an inch from your little shoe,
   Under the shade of the self-same tree)!
   Then I thought, 'Was there ever a maid so sweet?
And sweet will she be when her hair is gray,
   And the years shall have deadened her dear eyes' blue!'
But your mind was a thousand miles away,
   As, leaning back in your garden chair,
You counted your stitches and thought of him,
Whilst I could have sung out my soul for you!

(1880)

Emily Hickey

(IRELAND AND ENGLAND, 1845–1924)

'For Richer, For Poorer'

'Oh, give us of your oil, our lamps go out;
   Your well-fed lamps are clear and bright to see;
   And, if we go to buy us oil, maybe,
Far off our ears shall hear the jubilant shout,
"Behold the Bridegroom cometh, zoned about
   With utter light and utter harmony":
   Then leave us not to weep continually
In darkness, for our souls' hunger and drought.'

Then turned one virgin of the virgins wise
   To one among the foolish, with a low
Sweet cry, and looked her, lovelike, in the eyes,
    Saying, 'My oil is thine; for weal, for woe,
    We two are one, and where thou goest I go,
One lot being ours for aye, where'er it lies.'

(1889)

I Think of You as of a Good Life-boat

I think of you as of a good life-boat
That, once a-launch, thrilled aye and throbbed to meet
The mastered waves against her bow to beat,
And leap to the great ocean full afloat,
Where, wild about the sharp rocks of the world,
There was a storm of angry spray upswirled,
As passionate hands, in wan hope's struggles fierce,
Beat the strong waves till foam arose on foam,
Yet drew them none the nearer life and home.
And oh, to save them from the loss and curse,
And snatch them from the moaning deep, and bring
Safe to the quiet place of sheltering!

You have ceased to ride the storm, who breasted well
The dreadful surges and the tempest's swell;
Who brought the wrecked from terror of the sea
Into the haven where they fain would be.

Oh, well for you, and yet alas for me!

(1896)

'Michael Field'
(Katharine Bradley, ENGLAND, 1846–1914
and Edith Cooper, ENGLAND, 1862–1913)

'Atthis, my darling, thou did'st stray'

Atthis, my darling, thou did'st stray
A few feet to the rushy bed,
When a great fear and passion shook
My heart lest haply* thou wert dead;
It grew so still about the brook,
As if a soul were drawn away.

Anon thy clear eyes, silver-blue,
Shone through the tamarisk-branches fine;
To pluck me iris thou had'st sprung
Through galingale and celandine;
Away, away, the flowers I flung
And thee down to my breast I drew.

My darling! Nay, our very breath
Nor light nor darkness shall divide;
Queen Dawn shall find us on one bed,
Nor must thou flutter from my side
An instant, lest I feel the dread,
Atthis, the immanence of death.

(1889)

* haply: by any chance.

'Nought to me! So I choose to say'

Nought to me! So I choose to say:
We meet, old friends, about the bay;
The golden pulse grows on the shore –
Are not all things as heretofore
Now we have cast our love away?

Men throng us; thou art nought to me,
Therefore, indifferent, I can see
Within thine eyes the bright'ning grace
That once thou gavest face to face;
'Tis natural they welcome thee!

Nought to me, like the silver ring,
Thy mislaid, worthless gift. Last spring,
As any careless girl, I lost
The pin, yet, by the tears it cost,
It should have been worth cherishing.

Nought, nought! and yet if thou dost pass
I grow as summer-coloured grass,
And if I wrap my chiton* round,
I know thine ear hath caught the sound,
Although thou heedest not, alas!

Nought to me! Wherefore dost thou throw
On me that glittering glance, as though,
Friend, I had ever done thee wrong,
When the crowd asks me for the song,
'Atthis, I loved thee long ago'?

(1889)

* chiton: tunic.

'Beloved, now I love God first'

Beloved, now I love God first
There is for thee such summer burst
Where it was stirring spring before,
Lo, for thy feet a blossom-floor!

Patience! A little while to wait
Till I possess my new estate,
Then to assume thy glorious part
In my enriched and feasting heart.

(wr. 1907, pub. 1930)

Lovers

Lovers, fresh plighting lovers in our age
Lovers in Christ – so tender at the heart
The pull about the strings as they engage –
One thing is plain: – that we can never part.
O Child, thou hauntest me in every room;
Not for an instant can we separate;
And thou or I, if absent in a tomb
Must keep unqualified our soul's debate.
Death came to me but just twelve months ago
Threatening thy life; I counted thee as dead –
Christ by the bier took pity of my woe
And lifted thee and on my bosom spread;
And did not then retire and leave us twain:
Together for a little while we stood
And looked on Him, and chronicled His pain,
The wounds for us that started in their blood –
We, with one care, our common days shall spend,
As on that noble sorrow we attend.

(wr. 1912, pub. 1930)

'I am thy charge, thy care!'

I am thy charge, thy care!
Thou art praying for me, and about my bed,
About my ways; but there are things one misses –
   It is the little cup
   That I drink up,
The cup full of thee, offered every day –
I come for it, as birds draw to a brook –
It is the reflex of thee, in thy nook,
Caught sideways in a mirror as I pray –
   My precious Heap,
My jewel, in the casket of thy sleep.
Beloved, it is the little wreath of kisses,
I wove about thy head, thy withering hair.

(wr. 1914, pub. 1930)

Annie Hindle

(ENGLAND AND USA, *c.* 1847–after 1897)

Her Gift

'Oh give me that you prize the most,
   To prove your love sincere;
Whate'er is precious to your heart;
Something with which you would not part
   Except to one most dear.'

I looked upon her glowing face,
   And proffered this request;
'Twas but a passing whim of mine,
That she should give the sweetest sign,
   That I her heart possessed.

She drew the bracelet from her arm;
　'Take this, my love,' she said;
'It is the richest thing I own,
Though valued not for gold alone;
　'Twas worn by one now dead.'

I shook my head, and would not take
　The glittering armlet;
But clasped it on her arm again;
'Oh love, such gift would cause me pain,
　In causing you regret.'

'Then, here's a ring,' she murmured soft,
　''Tis neither rich nor new;
Oh, prithee, this dear token take,
And wear it for the giver's sake,
　Who gives her heart to you.'

'Nay, dearest, all these trifles keep,
　And grant me, I beseech,
Some bliss that wealth could never buy,
Some bliss that love would not deny
　To my imploring speech.'

She raised her face, until her eyes
　Were level with my own;
And with a blush, and roguish smile,
That said: – 'I meant to all the while,'
　Her loving arms were thrown

About my neck; the while her face
　Was in a brief eclipse;
And then, and there she gave, I know,
The sweetest gift she could bestow: –
　Her heart was on her lips!

(1871)

Edith Thomas

(USA, 1854–1925)

The Deep-Sea Pearl

The love of my life came not
   As love unto others is cast;
For mine was a secret wound –
   But the wound grew a pearl, at last.

The divers may come and go,
   The tides, they arise and fall;
The pearl in its shell lies sealed,
   And the Deep Sea covers all.

(before 1926)

Lizette Woodworth Reese

(USA, 1856–1935)

Nocturne

Topple the house down, wind;
Break it and tear it, rain;
She is not within,
Nor will come again.

That not even her ghost
Will know it for her own; –
Topple it into dust,
Tear it bone from bone.

(1926)

To a Dead Friend

To lose a lodging, yet to find the sky
House me more closely than all else I knew,
This did you going for me, friend; for you
Were all my loss, and yet the gainer I.
You forced me to the stars; this being so,
I have you, them, and also the high sun.
Your dreams for me, I dream them every one,
To prove me worth you, and the road I go.
Your nearness baffled me; I went amiss.
A rose across the thin width of a lane,
Is better known than one within the hand;
You see five petals, each sweet that or this.
The distance now between us makes you plain,
And your whole loveliness I understand.

(1926)

A. Mary F. Robinson

(ENGLAND, BELGIUM, ITALY AND FRANCE, 1857–1944)

Rosa Rosarum

Give me, O friend, the secret of thy heart
    Safe in my breast to hide,
So that the leagues which keep our lives apart
    May not ever our souls divide.

Give me the secret of thy life to lay
    Asleep within my own,
Nor dream that it shall mock thee any day
    By any sign or tone.

Nay, as in walking through some convent-close,
   Passing beside a well,
Oft have we thrown a red and scented rose
   To watch it as it fell;

Knowing that never more the rose shall rise
   To shame us, being dead;
Watching it spin and dwindle till it lies
   At rest, a speck of red –

Thus, I beseech thee, down the silent deep
   And darkness of my heart,
Cast thou a rose; give me a rose to keep,
   My friend, before we part.

For, as thou passest down thy garden-ways,
   Many a blossom there
Groweth for thee: lilies and laden bays,
   And rose and lavender.

But down the darking well one only rose
   In all the year is shed;
And o'er that chill and secret wave it throws
   A sudden dawn of red.

(1886)

Edith Nesbit

(ENGLAND, FRANCE AND GERMANY, 1858–1924)

To Vera, Who Asked a Song

If I only had time!
I could make you a rhyme.
But my time is kept flying
By smiling and sighing
  And living and dying for you.
The song-seed, I sow it,
I water and hoe it,
But never can grow it.
Ah, traitress, you know it!
  What is a poor poet to do?
Ah, let me take breath!
I am harried to death
By the loves and the graces
That crowd where your face is
  That lurk in your laces and throng.
Call them off for a minute,
Once let me begin it
The devil is in it
If I cannot spin it
  As sweet as a linnet, your song!

(1905)

Katharine Lee Bates

(USA, 1859–1929)

'Even as this globe shall gleam and disappear'

Even as this globe shall gleam and disappear
My life has vanished, life of joy I led
Folded in yours. Never again to tread
The station platform, tired scrutineer
Of every face, until a sudden cheer
Tingles through all my veins, fatigue is sped,
For you are with me, sweet as daily bread,
Refreshing as cool water! oh, the mere
Touch of your hand, your hand that is now ashes,
Turned all the day's vexations into mirth.
Beside you in the car, its groaning pull
And grinding brakes and harsh metallic crashes
Made blither music than remains on earth;
And yet I wonder I am sorrowful.

(1922)

Mary Coleridge

(ENGLAND, 1861–1907)

The Witch

I have walked a great while over the snow,
And I am not tall nor strong.
My clothes are wet, and my teeth are set,
And the way was hard and long.

I have wandered over the fruitful earth,
But I never came here before.
Oh, lift me over the threshold, and let me in at the door!

The cutting wind is a cruel foe.
I dare not stand in the blast.
My hands are stone, and my voice a groan,
And the worst of death is past.
I am but a little maiden still,
My little white feet are sore.
Oh, lift me over the threshold, and let me in at the door!

Her voice was the voice that women have,
Who plead for their heart's desire.
She came – she came – and the quivering flame
Sank and died in the fire.
It never was lit again on my hearth
Since I hurried across the floor,
To lift her over the threshold, and let her in at the door!

(1896)

Mistaken

I never thought that you could mourn
    As other women do.
A blossom from your garland torn,
A jewel dropped that you had worn,
    What could that be to you?

You never heard the human sound
    Of wailing and despair.
Nor faithful proved nor faithless found,
You lived and moved in beauty crowned,
    Content with being fair.

If I had known those eyes could weep
    That used to sparkle so,
You had been mine to love, to keep,
But all too late I probed the deep
    And all too late I knew.

(wr. 1888, pub. 1908)

Marriage

No more alone sleeping, no more alone waking,
    Thy dreams divided, thy prayers in twain;
Thy merry sisters to-night forsaking,
    Never shall we see thee, maiden, again.

Never shall we see thee, thine eyes glancing,
    Flashing with laughter and wild in glee,
Under the miseltoe kissing and dancing,
    Wantonly free.

There shall come a matron walking sedately,
    Low-voiced, gentle, wise in reply.
Tell me, O tell me, can I love her greatly?
    All for her sake must the maiden die!

(1900)

Not Yet

Time brought me many another friend
    That loved me longer.
New love was kind, but in the end
    Old love was stronger.

Years come and go. No New Year yet
   Hath slain December.
And all that should have cried – 'Forget!'
   Cries but – 'Remember!'

(1885)

Gone

About the little chambers of my heart
Friends have been coming – going – many a year.
   The doors stand open there.
Some, lightly stepping, enter; some depart.

Freely they come and freely go, at will.
The walls give back their laughter; all day long
   They fill the house with song.
One door alone is shut, one chamber still.

(1896)

Regina

My Queen her sceptre did lay down,
She took from her head the golden crown
Worn by right of her royal birth.
Her purple robe she cast aside,
And the scarlet vestures of her pride,
That was the pride of the earth.
In her nakedness was she
Queen of the world, herself and me.

My Queen took up her sceptre bright,
Her crown more radiant than the light,
The rubies gleaming out of the gold.
She donned her robe of purple rare,
And did a deed that none may dare,
That makes the blood run cold.
And in her bravery is she
Queen of herself, the world and me.

(1896)

'O let me be in loving nice'*

O let me be in loving nice,
Dainty, fine, and o'er precise,
That I may charm my charmèd dear
As tho' I felt a secret fear
To lose what never can be lost,
Her faith who still delights me most!
So shall I be more than true,
Ever in my ageing new.
So dull habit shall not be
Wrongly called Fidelity.

(wr. 1897, pub. 1908)

* nice: subtle or fastidious.

Hush

She sleeps so lightly, that in trembling fear
   Beside her, where she lies asleep, I kneel,
The rush of thought and supplication staying,
Lest by some inward sense she see and hear,
   If I too clearly think, too loudly feel,
And break her rest by praying.

(1890)

'Only a little shall we speak of thee'

Only a little shall we speak of thee,
   And not the thoughts we think;
There, where thou art – and art not – words would be
   As stones that sink.

We shall not see each other for thy face,
   Nor know the silly things we talk upon.
Only the heart says, 'She was in this place,
   And she is gone.'

(1902)

Sophie Jewett

(USA, ENGLAND AND ITALY, 1861–1909)

A Letter

The last light falls across your pictured face
(Unanswering sweet face, half turned away),
Withdrawing still, as down the west apace
Fades too the profile of June's longest day.
I wonder, did you watch an hour ago
While dropped the sun behind the mountain line?
And did you think how it, retreating so,
Must blaze along this level world of mine?
Love, what have I to do with sunset skies,
How red soever? All the world for me
Spreads eastward, and before my spirit's eyes,
Set fair between the mountains and the sea,
Doth stand the distant city of my heart.

Forgive me if I tell myself in vain:
'There is no power in this wide world to part
Our souls. Avail not time nor space nor pain,
For love is unconditioned.' Dear, to-night,
I am like an unlessoned child, who cries
For the sweet sensual things of touch and sight;
I want to read the gladness in your eyes;
I want your voice though but to speak my name;
My heart uncomforted, unsatisfied,
Hath put my best philosophy to shame.

Yet if you crossed the shadows to my side, –
No vision, but your very self indeed, –
I should not ask what kindly fate had brought
My heart's desire. I should not find at need
Expression for one eager waiting thought,

Not one of all the words I have to say.
I should but lean my cheek upon your hand,
And hold you close, the old, mute, childish way,
And you would comfort me and understand.

But not to-night, – I will be patient, Sweet,
Sit silently, and let life have its will.
The tread of the last passer in the street
Sounds with the chiming hour, then all is still,
Save that the little fountain in the park
Sings lazily the same old summer song
You knew in quiet nights when winds lay furled.
I needs must dream alone here in the dark
A little while, to-morrow go forth strong,
Lifting the shield of Love against the world.

(1896)

For a Birthday

Cornelia Frances Bates, Aet. * *79*

Long ago sweet songs were sung
Of fair ladies ever young;
Weary years of war might be,
Wearier wanderings over sea,
Exile in sad lands and strange,
Yet their beauty might not change.
Not a single word is told
Of a Helen who grows old;
Not her thousand sorrows dare
Dull the light of Deirdre's hair;
Iseult, lovelier than report,
Maiden in her father's court,

* *Aet.*: aged.

Grown world-radiant shall be seen
Through all time, Iseult the Queen.

Deirdre, Helen, Iseult are
Fadeless, shining star by star;
If their poets I might bring,
Skilled to touch the harp and sing,
Lady, I could bid them praise
Your brave crown of golden days;
Blithe and sweet their songs should be, –
Song of her who graciously
With each soft year younger grows,
As the earth with every rose.

(1908)

Louise Guiney

(USA AND ENGLAND, 1861–1920)

Private Theatricals

You were a haughty beauty, Polly
   (That was in the play),
I was the lover melancholy
   (That was in the play);
And when your fan and you receded,
And all my passion lay unheeded,
If still with tenderer words I pleaded,
   They were in the play.

I met my rival in the gateway
   (That was in the play),
And so we fought a duel straightway
   (That was in the play);

But when Jack hurt my arm unduly,
And you rushed over, softened newly,
And kissed me, Polly! truly, truly,
    Was that in the play?

(1884)

Amy Levy
(ENGLAND, 1861–89)

London in July

What ails my senses thus to cheat?
    What is it ails the place,
That all the people in the street
    Should wear one woman's face?

The London trees are dusty-brown
    Beneath the summer sky;
My love, she dwells in London town,
    Nor leaves it in July.

O various and intricate maze,
    Wide waste of square and street;
Where, missing through unnumbered days,
    We twain at last may meet!

And who cries out on crowd and mart?
    Who prates of stream and sea?
The summer in the city's heart —
    That is enough for me.

(1889)

To Lallie

(Outside the British Museum)

Up those Museum steps you came,
And straightaway all my blood was flame,
        Oh Lallie, Lallie!

The world (I had been feeling low)
In one short moment's space did grow
        A happy valley.

There was a friend, my friend, with you;
A meagre dame, in peacock blue
        Apparelled quaintly:

This poet-heart went pit-a-pat;
I bowed and smiled and raised my hat;
        You nodded – faintly.

My heart was full as full could be;
You had not got a word for me,
        Not one short greeting;

That nonchalant small nod you gave
(The tyrant's motion to the slave)
        Sole mark'd our meeting.

Is it so long? Do you forget
That first and last time that we met?
        The time was summer;

The trees were green; the sky was blue;
Our host presented me to you –
        A tardy comer.

You look'd demure, but when you spoke
You made a little, funny joke,
        Yet half pathetic.

Your gown was grey, I recollect,
I think you patronized the sect
    They call 'aesthetic'.*

I brought you strawberries and cream,
I plied you long about a stream
    With duckweed laden;

We solemnly discussed the – heat.
I found you shy and very sweet,
    A rosebud maiden.

Ah me, to-day! You passed inside
To where the marble gods abide:
    Hermes, Apollo,

Sweet Aphrodite, Pan; and where,
For aye reclined, a headless fair
    Beats all fairs hollow.

And I, I went upon my way,
Well – rather sadder, let us say;
    The world looked flatter.

I had been sad enough before,
A little less, a little more,
    What *does* it matter?

(1884)

---

* 'aesthetic': the Aesthetic Movement of the 1880s promoted soft draperies
in a pseudo-medieval or Greek style, worn without crinolines or corsets, as
in Pre-Raphaelite paintings.

At a Dinner Party

With fruit and flowers the board is decked,
  The wine and laughter flow;
I'll not complain – could one expect
  So dull a world to know?

You look across the fruit and flowers,
  My glance your glances find. –
It is our secret, only ours,
  Since all the world is blind.

(1889)

Charlotte Mew

(ENGLAND, 1869–1928)

On the Road to the Sea

We passed each other, turned and stopped for half an hour,
            then went our way,
  I who can make other women smile did not make you –
But no man can move mountains in a day.
  So this hard thing is yet to do.

But first I want your life: – before I die I want to see
  The world that lies behind the strangeness of your eyes,
There is nothing gay or green there for my gathering, it may be,
    Yet on brown fields there lies
A haunting purple bloom: is there not something in grey skies
      And in grey sea?
  I want what world there is behind your eyes,
  I want your life and you will not give it me.

Now, if I look, I see you walking down the years,
Young, and through August fields – a face, a thought, a
      swinging dream perched on a stile –;
I would have liked (so vile we are!) to have taught you tears
    But most to have made you smile.

To-day is not enough or yesterday: God sees it all –
Your length on sunny lawns, the wakeful rainy nights –; tell
      me –; (how vain to ask), but it is not a question –
      just a call –;
Show me then, only your notched inches climbing up the
      garden wall,
    I like you best when you are small.

    Is this a stupid thing to say
    Not having spent with you one day?
No matter; I shall never touch your hair
Or hear the little tick behind your breast,
    Still it is there,
    And as a flying bird
Brushes the branches where it may not rest
    I have brushed your hand and heard
The child in you: I like that best
So small, so dark, so sweet; and were you also then too grave
    and wise?
    Always, I think. Then put your far off little hand in mine; –
      Oh! let it rest;
I will not stare into the early world beyond the opening eyes,
    Or vex or scare what I love best.
    But I want your life before mine bleeds away –
      Here – not in heavenly hereafters – soon –
      I want your smile this very afternoon,
    (The last of all my vices, pleasant people used to say,
      I wanted and I sometimes got – the Moon!)

You know, at dusk, the last bird's cry,
And round the house the flap of the bat's low flight,
   Trees that go black against the sky
And then – how soon the night!

No shadow of you on any bright road again,
And at the darkening end of this – what voice? whose kiss? As
         if you'd say!
It is not I who have walked with you, it will not be I who take
         away
   Peace, peace, my little handful of the gleaner's grain
   From your reaped fields at the shut of day.

      Peace! Would you not rather die
      Reeling, – with all the cannons at your ear?
         So, at least, would I,
      And I may not be here
      To-night, tomorrow morning or next year.
      Still will I let you keep your life a little while,
            See dear?
         I have made you smile.

(1921)

Rooms

I remember rooms that have had their part
In the steady slowing down of the heart.
The room in Paris, the room at Geneva,
The little damp room with the seaweed smell,
And that ceaseless maddening sound of the tide –
Rooms where for good or for ill – things died.
But there is the room where we (two) lie dead,
Though every morning we seem to wake and might
      just as well seem to sleep again

As we shall somewhere in the other quieter,
        dustier bed
Out there in the sun – in the rain.

(pub. 1929)

Eva Gore-Booth

(IRELAND, ENGLAND AND ITALY, 1870–1926)

The Vision of Niamh

Life grows so clear, beneath the dreaming lamp,
I can see through the darkness of the grave,
How, long ago in her high mountain camp
The stars shone on the stormy soul of Maeve.

And leaning from the shadow of a star
With hands outstretched to hold the hands of clay,
One looked into her spirit fairer far
Than sun or moon of any mortal day.

Oh Niamh, thou art child of the dim hours
Between the day and night, when Summer flings
A little flashing dew on the wild flowers,
And all the starlight glimmers in thy wings.

Thou sorrow of lost beauty, thou strange queen
Who calls to men's soul of twilight seas,
Whose white hands break the stars in silver sheen,
Whose voice is as the wind in the fir trees.

For thee Maeve left her kingdom and her throne,
And all the gilded wisdom of the wise,
And dwelt among the hazel trees alone
So that she might look into Niamh's eyes.

No sorrow of lost battles any more
In her enchanted spirit could abide;
Straight she forgot the long and desolate war,
And how Fionavar for pity died.

Ah, Niamh, still the starry lamp burns bright,
I can see through the darkness of the grave,
How long ago thy soul of starry light
Was very dear to the brave soul of Maeve.

(1912)

The Travellers

To E. G. R.

Were it not strange that by the tideless sea
The jar and hurry of our lives should cease?
That under olive boughs we found our peace,
And all the world's great song in Italy?

Is it not strange though Peace herself has wings
And long ago has gone her separate ways,
On through the tumult of our fretful days
From Life to Death the great song chimes and rings?

In that sad day shall then the singing fail,
Shall Life go down in silence at the end,
And in the darkness friend be lost to friend,
And all our love and dreams of no avail?

You whose Love's melody makes glad the gloom
Of a long labour and a patient strife,
Is not that music greater than our life?
Shall not a little song outlast that doom?

(1904)

Florence Converse

(USA, 1871–1967)

Friendship

I

How strange a thing was friendship, long ago,
    When Shakespeare wrote those sonnets to his friend,
    Those passion sighings that begin and end
To sing one soul a song of love, – to show
That even a Shakespeare rather cared to know
    His other self had touched a joy, than spend
    One hour in striving how world's woe might mend.
Ah, would you that your friend should love you so?
Holding a lonely revel in your heart,
    And lifting careless laughter loud above
        The weeping of those very many true
Starved lovers she had lacked without – apart?
    No! say again the lesson of our love,
        And I will say it over after you.

II

We are not called to love that old, one way
    Our mothers used; that way the poets sing,
    Dan* Cupid's way, that blots out everything
Save you and me and love. This latter day
Unlearns us of our old love-lesson; nay,
    Not all of us, but our two selves, that bring
    Such wistful hearts to school, unmurmuring.
That way, we are not called to love, I say, –

* Dan: Sir or Master.

And say, and say; yet seems I am so slow
   To learn, so lingering laggard slow to lift
      The love-gates of my heart and let the flood
Race down the world. Be patient, yes, I know,
   From that close, niggard way we've cut adrift,
      But – 'tis the old tradition in my blood.

(1897)

Amy Lowell

(USA, 1874–1925)

The Letter

Little cramped words scrawling all over the paper
Like draggled fly's legs,
What can you tell of the flaring moon
Through the oak leaves?
Or of my uncurtained window and the bare floor
Spattered with moonlight?
Your silly quirks and twists have nothing in them
Of blossoming hawthorns,
And this paper is dull, crisp, smooth, virgin of loveliness
Beneath my hand.

I am tired, Beloved, of chafing my heart against
The want of you;
Of squeezing it into little inkdrops,
And posting it.
And I scald alone, here, under the fire
Of the great moon.

(1919)

A Shower

That sputter of rain, flipping the hedgerows
And making the highways hiss,
How I love it!
And the touch of you upon my arm
As you press against me that my umbrella
May cover you.
Tinkle of drops on stretched silk.
Wet murmur through green branches.

(1919)

April

A bird chirped at my window this morning,
And over the sky is drawn a light network of clouds.
Come,
Let us go out into the open,
For my heart leaps like a fish that is ready to spawn.

I will lie under the beech-trees,
Under the grey branches of the beech-trees,
In a blueness of little squills and crocuses.
I will lie among the little squills
And be delivered of this overcharge of beauty,
And that which is born shall be a joy to you
Who love me.

(1919)

Decade

When you came, you were like red wine and honey,
And the taste of you burnt my mouth with its sweetness.
Now you are like morning bread,
Smooth and pleasant.
I hardly taste you at all for I know your savour,
But I am completely nourished.

(1919)

Ursula Bethell

(NEW ZEALAND, ENGLAND, SWITZERLAND AND GERMANY,
1874–1945)

Discipline

I said: I will go into the garden and consider roses;
I will observe the deployment of their petals,
And compare one variety with another.
But I was made to sit down and scrape potatoes.

The morning's rosebuds passed by unattended,
While I sat bound to monotonous kitchen industry.
Howbeit the heart of my consort was exhilarated,
And for virtuous renunciation I received praise.

The taste of the potatoes was satisfactory
With a sprig of fresh mint, dairy butter, and very young green
    peas.

(1929)

Fortune

'At least we shall have roses,' laughed my companion,
Looking on the bundles arrived from the nursery;
All with their labels tied up so neatly,
All with their shaven crests and roots so well developed –
'We shall always have roses here.'

'At least we shall have roses,' this morning I repeated,
Looking on the summer's lustrous assemblage,
Beholding their long shoots, as once before in spring-time,
Zestfully preparing for their latter blooming –
'We shall always have roses, here.'

Others may sail away to the sea-coasts of Bohemia,
Cathay, and Coromandel, Malay, and Patagonia,
Hong Kong, and Halifax, Bombay, and Pernambuco,
Frisco and Singapore, and all the world's fine harbours –
Wistfully we may watch them loosed from our limitations, –
But for us, at least, roses, here.

(1929)

Gertrude Stein

(USA AND FRANCE, 1874–1946)

from Lifting Belly (II)

Kiss my lips. She did.

Kiss my lips again she did.

Kiss my lips over and over and over again she did.

I have feathers.

Gentle fishes.

Do you think about apricots. We find them very beautiful. It is
not alone their colour it is their seeds that charm us. We
find it a change.

Lifting belly is so strange.

I came to speak about it.

Selected raisins well their grapes grapes are good.

Change your name.

Question and garden.

It's raining. Don't speak about it.

My baby is a dumpling. I want to tell her something.

Wax candles. We have bought a great many wax candles.
Some are decorated. They have not been lighted.

I do not mention roses.

Exactly.

Actually.

Question and butter.

I find the butter very good.

Lifting belly is so kind.

Lifting belly fattily.

Doesn't that astonish you.

You did want me.

Say it again.

Strawberry.
Lifting beside belly.
Lifting kindly belly.
Sing to me I say.

(wr. 1915–17, pub. 1953)

Isabel Ecclestone Mackay

(CANADA, 1875–1928)

The Meeting

She flitted by me on the stair –
A moment since I knew not of her.
A look, a smile – she passed! but where
She flitted by me on the stair
Joy cradled exquisite despair;
For who am I that I should love her?
She flitted by me on the stair –
A moment since I knew not of her!

(1922)

Helen Hay Whitney

(USA, 1875–1944)

XXII: To a Woman

Take all of me, pour out my life as wine,
    To dye your soul's sweet shallows. Violent sin
    Blazed me a path, and I have walked therein,
Strong, unashamed. Your timorous hands need mine,

As the white stars their sky, your lips' pale line
　Shall blush to roses where my lips have been.
　I ask no more. I do not hope to win –
Only to add myself to your design.

Take all of me. I know your little lies,
Your light dishonor, gentle treacheries.
　I know, I lie in torment at your feet,
Shadow to all your sun. Take me and go,
　Use my adoring to your honor, sweet,
Strength for your weakness – it is better so.

(1905)

Natalie Barney

(USA, FRANCE AND ITALY, 1876–1972)

Habit

Ah! habit, how unmusical and shy
That outworn miracle: our ecstasy!
Between our hands that clasp their empty palms
This daily prayer is this our psalm of psalms!
What is this nothing that was more than all?
Thinned as a golden ring that dare not fall,
That unsuspected danger: faithfulness,
Has linked us strangers, and a something less!
Exchanging vows and other platitudes,
As beggars chained in separate solitudes,
Though jealousy keep live the rotten core,
Lovers that were be lovers nevermore.

(1920)

Angelina Weld Grimké
(USA, 1880–1958)

Rosabel

I

Leaves, that whisper, whisper ever,
    Listen, listen, pray;
Birds, that twitter, twitter softly,
    Do not say me nay;
Winds, that breathe about, upon her,
    (Since I do not dare)
Whisper, twitter, breathe unto her
    That I find her fair.

II

Rose whose soul unfolds white petaled
    Touch her soul rose-white;
Rose whose thoughts unfold gold petaled
    Blossom in her sight;
Rose whose heart unfolds red petaled
    Quick her slow heart's stir;
Tell her white, gold, red my love is;
    And for her, – for her.

(pub. 1991)

Caprichosa

I

Little lady coyly shy
With deep shadows in each eye
Cast by lashes soft and long,
Tender lips just bowed for song,
And I oft have dreamed the bliss
Of the nectar in one kiss
   But 'tis clear
   That I fear
The white anger that can lie
In the depths of her veiled eye,
Little nose so bold and pert,
That I fear me she's a flirt
And her eyes and smile demure
Are intended for a lure,
Cruel, dainty, little lady.

II

Dimples too in cheek and chin
Deep'ning when the smiles begin
Dancing o'er her mystic face;
Tiny hands of fragile grace
Yet for me their mighty sway
May crush out the light of day.
   And her feet
   So discreet
Hoarding all the shades for sleep,
And in drinking their perfume
I sink down mid lotus-bloom,
Cruel, dainty, little lady.

III

On some days she's shy and sweet
Gentler maid 'twere hard to meet:
Other days a lady grand
Cold and hard to understand
Greets me with a haughty stare –
Seeing naught but empty air;
   If I fume
   At my doom
Bows her dusky head to weep
Till I humbly to her creep
Grovelling in the very dirt –
But she's laughing! Little flirt!
Then, when I am most forlorn,
Wishing I had ne'er been born,
Woos me with alluring eyes,
Cooing words, and monstrous sighs,
But, if my foot one step advances
Lightly, swiftly, from me dances,
Darting at me mocking glances,
Cruel, dainty, little lady.

(wr. 1901, pub. 1991)

Marjorie Pickthall

(ENGLAND AND CANADA, 1883–1922)

The Lost Friend

Lest I forget,
In house or town or street,
God a great want has set
In every soul I meet,
However sweet.

In every friend
Something falls short that she
In daily grace would lend
Of strength to me
Or charity.

It is not there,
To speech or silence wed,
The dear, desired air,
The eager tread,
The lifted head.

Love like the hills,
Lost kindness like the rain, –
From other late-born ills
Comes other pain,
But not that grief again.

(1927)

Sara Teasdale
(USA, 1884–1933)

Song

You bound strong sandals on my feet,
    You gave me bread and wine,
And sent me under sun and stars,
    For all the world was mine.

Oh, take the sandals off my feet,
    You know not what you do;
For all the world is in your arms,
    My sun and stars are you.

(1911)

'H. D.' (Hilda Doolittle)
(USA, ENGLAND AND AUSTRIA, 1886–1961)

At Baia

I should have thought
in a dream you would have brought
some lovely, perilous thing,
orchids piled in a great sheath,
as who would say (in a dream)
I send you this,
who left the blue veins
of your throat unkissed.

Why was it that your hands
(that never took mine)

your hands that I could see
drift over the orchid heads
so carefully,
your hands, so fragile, sure to lift
so gently, the fragile flower stuff –
ah, ah, how was it

You never sent (in a dream)
the very form, the very scent,
not heavy, not sensuous,
but perilous – perilous –
of orchids, piled in a great sheath,
and folded underneath on a bright scroll
some word:

Flower sent to flower;
for white hands, the lesser white,
less lovely of flower leaf

or

Lover to lover, no kiss,
no touch, but forever and ever this.

(1921)

Fragment Thirty-Six

I know not what to do: my mind is divided. – Sappho

I know not what to do,
my mind is reft:
is song's gift best?
is love's gift loveliest?
I know not what to do,
now sleep has pressed
weight on your eyelids.

Shall I break your rest,
devouring, eager?
is love's gift best?
nay, song's the loveliest:
yet were you lost,
what rapture
could I take from song?
what song were left?

I know not what to do:
to turn and slake
the rage that burns,
with my breath burn
and trouble your cool breath?
so shall I turn and take
snow in my arms?
(Is love's gift best?)
Yet flake on flake
of snow were comfortless,
did you lie wondering,
wakened yet unawake.

Shall I turn and take
comfortless snow within my arms?
press lips to lips
that answer not,
press lips to flesh
that shudders not nor breaks?
Is love's gift best?
shall I turn and slake
all the wild longing?
O I am eager for you!
as the Pleiads shake
white light in whiter water
so shall I take you?

My mind is quite divided,
my minds hesitate,
so perfect matched,
I know not what to do:
each strives with each
as two white wrestlers
standing for a match,
ready to turn and clutch
yet never shake muscle nor nerve nor tendon;
so my mind waits
to grapple with my mind,
yet I lie quiet,
I would seem at rest.

I know not what to do:
strain upon strain,
sound surging upon sound
makes my brain blind;
as a wave-line may wait to fall
yet (waiting for its falling)
still the wind may take
from off its crest,
white flake on flake of foam,
that rises,
seeming to dart and pulse
and rend the light,
so my mind hesitates
above the passion
quivering yet to break,
so my mind hesitates above my mind,
listening to song's delight.

I know not what to do:
will the sound break,
rending the night
with rift on rift of rose
and scattered light?
will the sound break at last
as the wave hesitant,
or will the whole night pass
and I lie listening awake?

(1924)

Elizabeth Daryush

(ENGLAND AND IRAN, 1887–1977)

Forbidden Love

For Constance

If you were not what I know you to be,
(my knight) whose tower of control baffles me,
outside whose bolted and defended gates,
wide-eyed but dumb, my wistful spirit waits,
as a mourner waits by a rock-sealed tomb
for one who comes not, nor can ever come;

if you did not as you do – if you came,
sallied out only a little, to claim
what you know is yours – then it would be I,
(as *I* know that *you* know) who'd fortify
perforce my dwelling, dart sternness at you,
fight you as now I have no need to do.

Were *your* love other than it is, and *my*
love other, they would either force or fly
the deadlock, and, so doing, each would kill
the other, that now from firm walls of will
look friendly, calmly, unafraid to face
even each other, from that high, safe place.

(1934)

Katherine Mansfield

(NEW ZEALAND, ENGLAND AND FRANCE, 1888–1923)

Friendship

When we were charming *Backfisch**
   With curls and velvet bows
We shared a charming kitten
   With tiny velvet toes.

It was so gay and playful;
   It flew like a woolly ball
From my lap to your shoulder –
   And, oh, it was so small,

So warm – and so obedient
   If we cried: 'That's enough!'
It lay and slept between us,
   A purring ball of fluff.

But now that I am thirty
   And she is thirty-one,
I shudder to discover
   How wild our cat has run.

* Backfisch: teenagers.

It's bigger than a Tiger,
  Its eyes are jets of flame,
Its claws are gleaming daggers,
  Could it have once been tame?

Take it away, I'm frightened!
  But she, with placid brow,
Cries: 'This is our Kitty-witty!
  Why don't you love her now?'

(wr. 1919, pub. 1939)

Dorothy Wellesley, Duchess of Wellington
(ENGLAND, 1889–1956)

Maiden Castle

At Maiden Castle in Dorset
I saw two skeletons revealed.
I do not know if they loved one another,
But they lay as lover with lover.

I do not know if under the June sun,
After two thousand years
These knew they had loved one another;
Close locked in a ruined wall
One lay upon the other's shoulder:
I do not know if they loved one another.

They stared upon the actual sky
When at last men came to dig them up,
To find one lying on the other's shoulder:
I do not know if they were loved and lover.

Who shall say who is loved and lover,
When the earth must uncover
Those who lie so, the unloved, the lover?

(1955)

Lesbia Harford

(AUSTRALIA, 1891–1927)

'I count the days until I see you, dear'

I count the days until I see you, dear,
But the days only.
I dare not reckon up the nights and hours
I shall be lonely.

But when at last I meet you, dearest heart,
How can it cheer me?
Desire has power to turn me into stone,
When you come near me.

I give my heart the lie against my will,
Seem not to see you,
Glance aside quickly if I meet your eye,
Love you and flee you.

(wr. 1913, pub. 1985)

'I can't feel the sunshine'

I can't feel the sunshine
Or see the stars aright
For thinking of her beauty
And her kisses bright.

She would let me kiss her
Once and not again.
Deeming soul essential,
Sense doth she disdain.

If I should once kiss her,
I would never rest
Till I had lain hour long
Pillowed on her breast.

Lying so, I'd tell her
Many a secret thing
God has whispered to me
When my soul took wing.

Would that I were Sappho,
Greece my land, not this!
There the noblest women,
When they loved, would kiss.

(wr. 1915, pub. 1985)

Edna St Vincent Millay
(USA, 1892–1950)

Evening on Lesbos*

Twice having seen your shingled heads adorable
Side by side, the onyx and the gold,
I know that I have had what I could not hold.

Twice have I entered the room, not knowing she was here.
Two agate eyes, two eyes of malachite,
Twice have been turned upon me, hard and bright.

* Lesbos: the Greek island famous as the birthplace of Sappho, from which
the word 'lesbian' derives.

Whereby I know my loss.
      Oh, not restorable
Sweet incense, mounting in the windless night!

(1928)

Vita Sackville-West

(ENGLAND, 1892–1962)

No Obligation

Come on the wings of great desire,
   Or stay away from me.
You're not more stable than the day,
   Or than the day less free.

The dawning day has clouds in store;
   Desire her cloudy moods;
And sunlit woods of morning may
   By noon be darkened woods.

So be you free to come or stay
   Without a reason given,
As free as clouds that blot the light
   Across the face of heaven.

(1932)

Sylvia Townsend Warner
(ENGLAND AND SPAIN, 1893–1978)
and Valentine Ackland
(ENGLAND, FRANCE AND SPAIN, 1906–68)

'The clock plods on –'

The clock plods on –
'She comes not, she comes not –'
(A stutter between words)
'She c-comes not –'
Under the hill the wind lurks for weather,
I sit alone.
The gulls driven inshore fly over and thither,
Hide they and hide I.
The clock plods onwards,
'She comes not, c-comes not –'
But now I am glad.
If I heard her step I should go like the birds,
Inshore and away –
At night and when storm-clouds are high
It is no time for play.
I know I am glad that she comes not –
If she came, and love's storm should arise –
What then –
With the gale outside, and within
A fiercer wind blowing?
If she came with the storm in her eyes
There's no knowing.

(VA, 1934)

'The eyes of the body, being blindfold by night'

The eyes of the body, being blindfold by night
Refer to the eyes of mind – at brain's command
Study imagination's map, then order out a hand
To journey forth as deputy for sight.

Thus and by these ordered ways
I come at you – Hand deft and delicate
To trace the suavely laid and intricate
Route of your body's maze.

My hand, being deft and delicate, displays
Unerring judgment; cleaves between your thighs
Clean, as a ray-directed airplane flies.

Thus I, within these strictly ordered ways,
Although blindfolded, seize with more than sight
Your moonlit meadows and your shadowed night.

(VA, 1934)

'Since the first toss of gale that blew'

Since the first toss of gale that blew
Me in to you
The wind that our still love awakened
Has never slackened,
But watchful with nightfall keeps pace
With each embrace.
If we love out the winter, my dear,
This will be a year
That babes now lulled on arm will quote
With rusty throat.

For long meeting of our lips
Shall be breaking of ships,
For breath drawn quicker men drowned
And trees downed.
Throe shall fell roof-tree, pulse's knock
Undermine rock,
A cry hurl seas against the land,
A raiding hand,
Scattering lightning along thighs
Lightning from skies
Wrench, and fierce sudden snows clamp deep
On earth our sleep.
Yet who would guess our coming together
Should breed wild weather
Who saw us now? – with looks as sure
As the demure
Flame of our candle, no more plied
By tempest outside
Than those deep ocean weeds unrecking
What winds, what wrecking
What wrath of wild our dangerous peace
Waits to release.

(STW, 1934)

Ruth Pitter

(ENGLAND, 1897–1992)

If You Came

If you came to my secret glade,
  Weary with heat,
I would set you down in the shade,
  I would wash your feet.

If you came in the winter sad,
  Wanting for bread,
I would give you the last that I had,
  I would give you my bed.

But the place is hidden apart
  Like a nest by a brook,
And I will not show you my heart
  By a word, by a look.

The place is hidden apart
  Like the nest of a bird:
And I will not show you my heart
  By a look, by a word.

(1939)

Old, Childless, Husbandless

Old, childless, husbandless, bereaved, alone,
She knew more love than any I have known.
Familiar with the sickness at its worst,
She smiled at the old woman she had nursed
So long; whose bed she shared, that she might hear
The threadbare whisper in the night of fear.

She looked, and saw the change. The dying soul
Smiled her last thanks, and passed. Then Mary stole
About the room, and did what must be done,
Unwilling, kind heart, to call anyone,
It was so late: all finished, down she lay
Beside the dead, and calmly slept till day.

Urania!* what could child or husband be
More than she had, to such a one as she?

(1939)

Antoinette Scudder

(USA, 1898–after 1949)

Tea making

My lady love
Is making tea – she strikes
A match and the shrill blue flame leaps up
While the kettle's polished round
Reflects her smiling face.

And then she dips
By such a slender chain
A silver ball in the steaming draught
That slowly turns from crystal pure
To amber golden brown.

Just so my heart
These many moons has swung
From her finger tip and bubbled and brewed
Such a strong, such a seething hot
Witch's drink of desire.

* Urania: goddess of spiritual love and beauty; 'Uranian' was a tactful
adjective for same-sex love in the first decade of the twentieth century.

And last of all,
She drops into the cup
A cube of sugar moon-white that melts
And crumbles away like my heart
Whenever she looks at me.

(before 1947)

Elsa Gidlow

(ENGLAND, CANADA AND USA, 1898–1986)

Relinquishment

Go her way, her quiet, quiet way.
Her way is best for one so wistful tired;
My three-months' lover, go with your world-sick heart,
Your love-bruised flesh. I am no sanctuary.

This hot mouth, these ardent, out-reaching arms,
This hollow between my breasts, these hungry limbs,
They are a cradle, a cradle of living flame,
No haven for you, saddening after peace.

I am not certain, no, nor soothing safe.
Mine is the shifting, perilous way of life.
Pitiless, ever-changing, hazardous,
My love insatiate and mutable.

Go her way, her quiet, well-path'd way.
Sit by her hearth-fire, let her keep you safe.
Mine the unharbored heart, the uncharted passions,
Mine at the end a more than common peace.

(1923)

Constancy

You're jealous if I kiss this girl and that,
You think I should be constant to one mouth?
Little you know of my too quenchless drouth:
My sister, I keep faith with love, not lovers.

Life laid a flaming finger on my heart,
Gave me an electric golden thread,
Pointed to a pile of beads and said:
Link me one more glorious than the rest.

Love's the thread, my sister, you a bead,
An ivory one, you are so delicate.
Those first burned ash-grey – far too passionate.
Further on the colors mount and sing.

When the last bead's painted with the last design
And slipped upon the thread, I'll tie it: so;
Then smiling quietly I'll turn and go
While vain Life boasts her latest ornament.

(1923)

Philosophy

Since we must soon be fed
As honey and new bread
To ever hungry Death:
O, love me very sweet
And kiss me very long
And let us use our breath
For song.
Nothing else endures
Overlong.

(1923)

Alice V. Stuart

(BURMA, SCOTLAND AND ENGLAND, 1899–1983)

The Plait of Hair

'Time has not laid
A finger on your loveliness,' I said,
'Still the same rose-wild face, the same bright toss
Of glowing hair.'
                Seated at your looking-glass
You smiled at me, and shook your exquisite head,
Reached in a drawer, and set
Above your brows, a red-gold coronet,
A plait of hair cut off six years ago.
'This is my hair as it was.'
                Against that glow
Your rich locks dimmed a trifle. How smooth, how slow
The shadow creeps on the dial!
                I, too soon,
Swearing your sun at noon,
Saw it had crossed its zenith, saw the shade
Had shifted, by one degree, to afternoon
And lengthening shadows.
                Time, the adroit thief, strips
So gradually the warmth of youth from lips
And cheek and hair, we are deceived. But you,
You marked the theft: you knew.

I loved you better for the laughing ruth
With which you faced your mirror, and the truth.

(pub. 1980)

Thelma Tyfield
(SOUTH AFRICA, 1906–68)

Gifts

You bring me (neighbourly)
sprays
of sweet-pea and
jasmine –

bring me (quite
unaware of it)
sprays
of yourself.
The gifts
have sweetened my house
and beckoned all
things – floral and
human – near me.

(1972)

Dorothy Livesay

(CANADA, *b.* 1909)

Arms And the Woman*

My hand within you
yours in me
by these crossed swords
we make a peace
not of this world
song without words

(1984)

May Sarton

(BELGIUM AND USA, 1912–95)

from The Autumn Sonnets

If I can let you go as trees let go
Their leaves, so casually, one by one;
If I can come to know what they do know,
That fall is the release, the consummation,
Then fear of time and the uncertain fruit
Would not distemper the great lucid skies
This strangest autumn, mellow and acute.
If I can take the dark with open eyes

---

* Arms And the Woman: this title offers a twist on 'I sing of arms and the
man', the first line of Virgil's twelve-book Latin epic, the *Aeneid*.

And call it seasonal, not harsh or strange
(For love itself may need a time of sleep),
And, treelike, stand unmoved before the change,
Lose what I lose to keep what I can keep,
The strong root still alive under the snow,
Love will endure – if I can let you go.

(1972)

After All These Years

After all these years
When all I could caress
Was dog head and dog ears
When all that came to bless
Was cat with her loud purrs,
With what joy and what quake
I kiss small naked ears
And stroke a marble cheek,
After all these years
Let sleeping beauty wake.

(1980)

Love

Fragile as a spider's web
Hanging in space
Between tall grasses,
It is torn again and again.

A passing dog
Or simply the wind can do it.
Several times a day
I gather myself together
And spin it again.

Spiders are patient weavers.
They never give up.
And who knows
What keeps them at it?
Hunger, no doubt,
And hope.

(1980)

May Swenson
(USA, 1913–89)

Poet to Tiger

The Hair

You went downstairs
saw a hair in the sink
and squeezed my toothpaste by the neck.
You roared. My ribs are sore.
This morning even my pencil's got your toothmarks.
Big Cat Eye cocked on me you see bird bones.
Snuggled in the rug of your belly
your breath so warm
I smell delicious fear.
Come breathe on me rough pard
put soft paws here.

The Salt

You don't put salt on anything
so I'm eating without.
Honey on the eggs is all right
mustard on the toast.
I'm not complaining I'm saying I'm
living with *you*.
You like your meat raw
don't care if it's cold.
Your stomach must have tastebuds
you swallow so fast.
Night falls early. It's foggy. Just now.

I found another of your bite marks in the cheese.
I'm hungry. Please
come bounding home
I'll hand you the wine to open
with your teeth.
Scorch me a steak unsalted
boil my coffee twice
say the blessing to a jingle on the blue TV.
Under the lap robe on our chilly couch
look behind my ears 'for welps'
and hug me.

The Sand

You're right I brought a grain
or two of sand
into bed I guess in my socks.
But it was you pushed them off
along with everything else.

Asleep you flip
over roll
everything under
you and off
me. I'm always grabbing
for my share of the sheets.

Or else you wake me every hour with sudden
growled I-love-yous
trapping my face between those plushy
shoulders. All my float-dreams turn spins
and never finish. I'm thinner
now. My watch keeps running fast.
But best is when we're riding pillion
my hips within your lap. You let me steer.
Your hand and arm go clear
around my ribs your moist
dream teeth fastened on my nape.

A grain of sand in the bed upsets you or
a hair on the floor.
But you'll get
in slick and wet from the shower if I let
you. Or with your wool cap
and skiing jacket on
if it's cold.
Tiger don't scold me
don't make me comb my hair outdoors.
Cuff me careful. Like don't
crunch. Make last what's yours.

The Dream

You get into the tub holding *The Naked Ape*
   in your teeth. You wet that blond
   three-cornered pelt lie back wide
     chest afloat. You're reading
    in the rising steam and I'm
drinking coffee from your tiger cup.
     You say you dreamed
     I had your baby book
    and it was pink and blue.
   I pointed to a page and there
  was your face with a cub grin.

You put your paws in your armpits
    make a tiger-moo.
   Then you say: 'Come here
     Poet and take
      this hair
     off me.' I do.
  It's one of mine. I carefully
    kill it and carry
   it outside. And stamp on it
    and bury it.
   In the begonia bed.
And then take off my shoes
   not to bring a grain
    of sand in to get
     into our bed.
    I'm going to
    do the cooking
    now instead
     of you.
  And sneak some salt in
  when you're not looking.

(1970)

Naomi Replansky

(USA AND FRANCE, *b.* 1918)

The Dangerous World

I watched you walk across the street,
Slightly stooped, not seeing me,
And smiled to see that mixture of
Clumsiness, grace, intensity.

Then suddenly I feared the cars,
The streets you cross, the days you pass.
You hold me as a glass holds water.
You can be shattered like a glass.

(1994)

Adrienne Rich

(USA, *b.* 1929)

from Twenty-One Love Poems

XVII

No one's fated or doomed to love anyone.
The accidents happen, we're not heroines,
they happen in our lives like car crashes,
books that change us, neighborhoods
we move into and come to love.
Tristan and Isolde is scarcely the story,
women at least should know the difference
between love and death. No poison cup,

no penance. Merely a notion that the tape-recorder
should have caught some ghost of us: that tape-recorder
not merely played but should have listened to us,
and could instruct those after us:
this we were, this is how we tried to love,
and these are the forces they had ranged against us,
and these are the forces we had ranged within us,
within us and against us, against us and within us.

(1978)

Maureen Duffy
(ENGLAND, *b.* 1933)

Eureka

Turning to sponge a flank
In the bath, a new manoeuvre
Out of laziness, flu, old age,
I discover a big brown mole
That you must often have met
And wonder what else you know
Of me secret from even myself,
What other blemishes of mind
Or body you caress lovingly
Behind my back.

(1971)

Audre Lorde

(USA AND MEXICO, 1934–92)

Love Poem

Speak earth and bless me
with what is richest
make sky flow honey out of my hips
rigid as mountains
spread over a valley
carved out by the mouth of rain

And I knew when I entered her   I was
high wind in her forest's hollow
fingers whispering sound
honey flowed   from the split cut
impaled on a lance of tongues
on the tips of her breasts   on her navel
and my breath   howling into her entrances
through lungs of pain.

Greedy as herring-gulls
or a child
I swing out over   the earth
over and over   again.

(1971)

Jane Chambers

(USA, 1938–83)

To Beth On Her Forty-Second Birthday

I sat up all night and watched you sleep. I did,
all night. At midnight you became a year older
but you didn't know it. Swathed in my childhood
quilt, where so many of my childhood dreams
were born, most of which you have made come
true. Or perhaps you did know. It was just about
midnight when you hooked your toes in the
anklets of your socks and pitched them across
the room, as though preparing to run through
the dewy new grass. You have certainly been the
finest and most perfect part of my life. But I
sometimes wonder what you might have become
without me, without me hanging around your
neck in relentless poverty. Might you have become
a rich woman? Without my constant suckling
for approval and need for support, might you
have found a creative avenue of your own?
    And so here I sit, watching you sleep, ex-
hausted from the day to day taking care of me
instead of bursting exuberant into this new and
important year of your life. Just don't remember
me like this. Remember when I could haul fifty
pounds of firewood into the house single-handed
and lift you off the floor with one arm. No matter
what happens, we have something that most
people never do: the best. Happy Birthday.
I love you forever.

(pub. 1984)

Judy Grahn

(USA, *b.* 1940)

'Ah, Love, you smell of petroleum'

Ah, Love, you smell of petroleum
and overwork
with grease on your fingernails,
paint in your hair
there is a pained look in your eye
from no appreciation
you speak to me of the lilacs
and appleblossoms we ought to have
the banquets we should be serving,
afterwards rubbing each other for hours
with tenderness and genuine
olive oil
someday. Meantime here is your cracked plate
with spaghetti. Wash your hands &
touch me, praise
my cooking. I shall praise your calluses.
we shall dance in the kitchen of our imagination.

(1977)

Suniti Namjoshi

(INDIA, USA, CANADA AND ENGLAND, *b.* 1941)

and Gillian Hanscombe

(AUSTRALIA AND ENGLAND, *b.* 1945)

'Well, then let slip the masks'

Well, then let slip the masks
    and all the notes we have taken,
let them fall to the ground and turn into petals
to make more luxurious our bed, or let them
turn into leaves and blow in the air, let them
make patterns, let them amuse themselves.
The curve of your breast is like the curve
of a wave: look, held, caught, each instant
caught, the wave tipping over and we in our bower,
the two of us sheltered, my hands on your thighs,
your body, your back, my mouth on your mouth
and in the hollows of your jaws and your head
nuzzling my breasts. And the wave above us is
folding over now, folding and laughing. Will you
take to the sea, my darling? Will you let me caress you?
The tips of your feet, your legs, your sex?
Will you let my tongue caress you? Will you
lie in my arms? Will you rest? And if the sun
is too strong, should burn too much, will you
walk with me to where the light is more calm
and be in me where the seas heave and are
serene and heave again and are themselves?

(1986)

Marilyn Hacker

(USA, ENGLAND AND FRANCE, *b.* 1942)

Coming Downtown

Lie down beside me if it's good for you.
I only had to see you face-to-face.
I won't stay if you don't want me to.

What is this crap we push each other through
the phone wires, through the length of rainy days?
Lie down beside me if it's good for you.

One last sarcastic curveball, that who threw
at whom, and who got stranded on third base?
I won't stay if you don't want me to,

but you didn't show up after, and I knew
a whole night might let wolves loose in our space.
Lie down beside me if it's good for you.

There'll be a cab on Second Avenue.
I'll have the driver bring me to your place.
I won't stay if you don't want me to

— but seeing you illuminates the true
path (for me) through the whole beast-ridden maze.
Lie down beside me if it's good for you

to hold me now. Another night will do
as well (I guess). Though what I'm feeling stays,
I won't stay unless you want me to . . .

A nightcap, or a quick 'Afore ye go'?
I need to know my need is no disgrace.
Lie down beside me if it's good for you.

But we avoided that scenario.
A sense of humour is a state of grace,
And I will stay, and I am going to
lie down beside you and be good for you.

(1986)

Daphne Marlatt

(CANADA, *b.* 1942)

Coming to you

through traffic, honking and off-course, direction veering
presently up your street, car slam, soon enough on my feet,
eager and hesitant, peering with the rush of coming to you,
late, through hydrangeas nodding out with season's age,
and roses open outline still the edge of summer gone in
grounding rain. elsewhere, or from it, i brush by, impa-
tient, bending to your window to surprise you in that place
i never know, you alone with yourself there, one leg on
your knee, you with boots, with headphones on, grave,
rapt with inaudible music. the day surrounds you: point
where everything listens. and i slow down, learning how to
enter – implicate and unspoken (still) heart-of-the-world.

(1984)

Pat Parker

(USA, 1944–89)

For Willyce

When i make love to you
  i try
    with each stroke of my tongue
      to say   i love you
      to tease i love you
      to hammer i love you
      to melt i love you

  & your sounds drift down
    oh god!
      oh jesus!
    and I think –
  here it is, some dude's
  getting credit for what
    a woman
    has done,
    again.

(1978)

Minnie Bruce Pratt

(USA, *b.* 1946)

Bury and Dig

We bury and dig each other up
for love. Sometimes it's like death,
sometimes like carrots: invisible
seeds delicately smoothed under,

a slow growth, filaments of hair
at the roots; grasping, pulling
at more hair, springy and leafy,
the cool length of your thigh,
a smell of red dirt under my nails.

Sometimes like beets: wintering over
under ground, the red heart waiting.

(1985)

Cheryl Clarke

(USA, *b.* 1947)

Nothing

Nothing I wouldn't do for the woman I sleep with
when nobody satisfy me the way she do.

kiss her in public places
win the lottery
take her in the ass
in a train lavatory
sleep three in a single bed
have a baby
to keep her wanting me

wear leather underwear
remember my dreams
make plans and schemes
go down on her in front of her
other lover
give my jewelry away
to keep her wanting me

sell my car
tie her to the bed post and
spank her
lie to my mother
let her watch me fuck my other lover
miss my only sister's wedding
to keep her wanting me

buy her cocaine
show her the pleasure in danger
bargain
let her dress me in colorful costumes
of low cleavage and slit to the crotch
giving her easy access
to keep her wanting me.

Nothing I wouldn't do for the woman I sleep with
when nobody satisfy me the way she do.

(1986)

Olga Broumas

(GREECE AND USA, *b.* 1949)

Song / for Sanna

. . . in this way the future enters
into us, in order to transform itself
in us before it happens
R. M. Rilke

What hasn't happened
intrudes, so much
hasn't yet happened. In the steamy

kitchens we meet in, kettles
are always boiling, water for tea, the steep
infusions we occupy
hands and mouth with, steam
filming our breath, a convenient

subterfuge, a disguise
for the now
sharp intake, the measured
outlet of air, the sigh, the gutting
loneliness

of the present where
what hasn't happened will
not be ignored, intrudes, separates
from the conversation like milk
from cream, desire

rising between the cups, brimming
over our saucers, clouding the minty
air, its own
aroma a pungent
stress, once again, you will get
up, put on your coat, go

home to the safer passions, moisture
clinging still to your spoon, as the afternoon
wears on, and I miss, I
miss you.

(1977)

Michèle Roberts

(ENGLAND, USA, ITALY AND FRANCE, *b.* 1949)

Magnificat

for Sian, after thirteen years

oh this man
what a meal he made of me
how he chewed and gobbled and sucked
in the end he spat me all out

you arrived on the dot, in the nick
of time, with your red curls flying
I was about to slip down the sink like grease
I nearly collapsed, I almost
wiped myself out like a stain
I called for you, and you came, you voyaged
fierce as a small archangel with swords and breasts
you declared the birth of a new life
in my kitchen there was an annunciation
and I was still, awed by your hair's glory

you commanded me to sing of my redemption

oh my friend, how
you were mother for me, and how
I could let myself lean on you
comfortable as an old cloth
familiar as enamel saucepans
I was a child again, pyjama'ed
in winceyette, my hair plaited, and you

listened, you soothed me like cake and milk
you listened to me for three days, and I poured
it out, I flowed all over you like wine, like oil
you touched the place where it hurt
at night, we slept together in my big bed
your shoulder eased me towards dreams

when we met, I tell you
it was a birthday party, a funeral
it was a holy communion
between women, a Visitation
it was two old she-goats butting
and nuzzling each other in the smelly fold

(1986)

Mary Dorcey

(IRELAND, ENGLAND, FRANCE, JAPAN AND USA, *b.* 1950)

Night

I remember your neck, its strength
and the sweetness of the skin at your throat.
I remember your hair, long, in our way
drawing it back from my mouth.
How my hands slid the low plain of your back
thrown by the sudden flaunt of your loins.
I remember your voice, the first low break
and at last the long flight
loosing us to darkness.
And your lips along my shoulder,
more sure, even than I had imagined –
how I guarded their track.

I ask you then what am I to do with all these
memories
heavy and full?
Hold them, quiet, between my two hands,
as I would if I could again
your hard breasts?

(1982)

Brenda Brooks

(CANADA, *b.* 1952)

Anything

I can be
your man, I can
be your mother,
I can be

your reluctant nun,

or your favourite
amphibian, fluent
on land or water.

I can be
the girl with
couldn't-care-less hair
who galloped her
best horse into
the schoolyard &
won your marbles
fair and square.

We could be
dirty & twelve
again, find some
trouble to be up to,
invent our own
words for things –
we could tell
them to each other
in the pungent,
private places
girls like us

(tree girls,
river girls,
girls with pine-cones
on their minds,
who tell time
by the sun, who
find their bearings
by the stars,
restless girls
whose bikes have hooves,
girls with bows
& arrows they made
themselves,
girls with
the sounds of horses
in their throats)

always find.

Fluent on land
or water,
we could be
man, or
mother.

(1990)

Dionne Brand

(TRINIDAD AND CANADA, *b.* 1953)

from hard against the soul

X

Then it is this simple. I felt the unordinary romance of
women who love women for the first time. It burst in
my mouth. Someone said this is your first lover, you
will never want to leave her. I had it in mind that I
would be an old woman with you. But perhaps I
always had it in mind simply to be an old woman,
then, I decided it was you when you found me in that
apartment drinking whisky for breakfast. When I came
back from Grenada and went crazy for two years, that
time when I could hear anything and my skin was
flaming like a nerve and the walls were like paper
and my eyes could not close. I suddenly sensed you
at the end of my room waiting. I saw your back arched
against this city we inhabit like guerillas, I brushed my
hand, conscious, against your soft belly, waking up.

(1990)

Carol Ann Duffy
(SCOTLAND AND ENGLAND, *b.* 1955)

Warming Her Pearls

Next to my own skin, her pearls. My mistress
bids me wear them, warm them, until evening
when I'll brush her hair. At six, I place them
round her cool, white throat. All day I think of her

resting in the Yellow Room, contemplating silk
or taffeta, which gown tonight? She fans herself
whilst I work willingly, my slow heat entering
each pearl. Slack on my neck, her rope.

She's beautiful. I dream about her
in my attic bed; picture her dancing
with tall men, puzzled by my faint, persistent scent
beneath her French perfume, her milky stones.

I dust her shoulders with a rabbit's foot,
watch the soft blush seep through her skin
like an indolent sigh. In her looking-glass
my red lips part as though I want to speak.

Full moon. Her carriage brings her home. I see
her every movement in my head ... Undressing,
taking off the jewels, her slim hand reaching
for the case, slipping naked into bed, the way

she always does ... And I lie here awake,
knowing the pearls are cooling even now
in the room where my mistress sleeps. All night
I feel their absence and I burn.

(1987)

Jackie Kay

(SCOTLAND AND ENGLAND, *b.* 1961)

Pounding Rain

News of us spreads like a storm.
The top of our town to the bottom.
We stand behind curtains
parted like hoods; watch each other's eyes.

We talk of moving to the west end,
this bit has always been a shoe box
tied with string; but then again
your father still lives in that house
where we warmed up spaghetti bolognese
in lunch hours and danced to Louis Armstrong,
his gramophone loud as our two heart beats
going boom diddy boom diddy boom.

Did you know then? I started dating Davy;
when I bumped into you I'd just say Hi.
I tucked his photo booth smile into my satchel
brought him out for my pals in the intervals.

A while later I heard you married Trevor Campbell.
Each night I walked into the school dinner hall
stark naked, till I woke to Miss, Miss, Miss
every minute. Then, I bumped into you at the Cross.

You haven't changed you said; that reassurance.
Nor you; your laugh still crosses the street.
I trace you back, beaming, till –
Why don't you come round, Trevor would love it.

He wasn't in. I don't know how it happened.
We didn't bother with a string of do you remembers.
I ran my fingers through the beads in your hair.
Your hair's nice I said stupidly, nice, suits you.

We sat and stared till our eyes filled
like a glass of wine. I did it, the thing
I'd dreamt a million times. I undressed you
slowly, each item of clothing fell
with a sigh. I stroked your silk skin
until we were back in the Campsies, running
down the hills in the pounding rain,
screaming and laughing; soaked right through.

(1991)

Ali Smith

(SCOTLAND AND ENGLAND, *b.* 1962)

Genesis

Imagine. You come easily to me
smoothly as honey comes around a spoon
as apples come easily to the tree.

I walk in trees, wake under trees alone,
imagine. You come easily to me
as honey to my mouth. I sit in sun.

As apples come easily to the tree
the summer sees this languid madness born.
Imagine. You come easily to me

a cooler midnight and the knowledge then
as apples come easily to the tree
your sapling spine, the strength of it, your skin

imagine. You come easily to me.
I did not think that I would fall so soon
as apples come easily to the tree

as easy as sky falls through leaves, blue green
as natural as rain in heat, as keen,
imagine. You come easily to me
as apples come easily to the tree.

(1990)

BIOGRAPHICAL NOTES

VALENTINE ACKLAND (1906–68) was educated in London, Norfolk and Paris. Her partnership with SYLVIA TOWNSEND WARNER began in 1930. They went to the Spanish Civil War as Red Cross volunteers, after which they became Communists. Once they had settled in Dorset, their enduring relationship was sometimes disrupted by Ackland's alcoholism and affairs with other women. Ackland wrote short stories, an exposé on English rural poverty and a painfully honest autobiography, *For Sylvia*. In her later years she returned to Catholicism before dying of breast cancer.

The poems included are from a joint collection of 1934 by Ackland and Warner, *Whether a Dove or a Seagull*.

Daughter of a tenant farmer, JANE BARKER (1652–*c*. 1727) grew up in Wilsthorpe, Lincolnshire, and learned medicine from her brother, who introduced her to his Cambridge academic friends. As a poet she modelled herself on KATHERINE PHILIPS. After her parents' deaths Barker converted to Catholicism and followed the court of James II to St Germain. Despite going blind, she continued to spy for the Jacobites while she published a handful of experimental, patchwork-style novels about an adventurous spinster.

After a European finishing school, NATALIE BARNEY (1876–1972) 'came out' as a débutante in Washington, DC. Her artist mother illustrated Natalie's first book of poetry; her father, shocked by its lesbian content, tried to suppress it by buying the plates. But she inherited the fortune he had made from the railroads, and at twenty-six settled for life in Paris, where she ran a famous salon at 20 rue Jacob and established an Académie des Femmes. She won more fame for her social life and many lovers than for her fiction, memoirs and poetry. Barney spent the Second World War in Italy, where she supported the Fascists. Radclyffe Hall portrayed her as a minor character in *The Well of Loneliness*.

KATHARINE LEE BATES (1859–1929) is best known for writing 'America the Beautiful'. From 1885 she was an Instructor in English Literature at Wellesley College, Massachusetts, living with a colleague, Katharine Coman, who died in 1915. Bates published college texts, travel books and stories for children, but placed most value on her six collections of poetry.

'Even as this globe shall gleam and disappear' is from 'In Bohemia: A Corona of Sonnets' which was published in *Yellow Clover*, a volume commemorating Katharine Coman which Bates gave their friends and colleagues as an Easter present in 1922. In the sonnet that follows this one, Bates wonders why she is 'sorrowful' since her beloved must be happier in heaven.

Lauded by Virginia Woolf as the first professional woman writer in England, APHRA BEHN (*c.* 1640–89) was an innkeeper's daughter who became a spy for Charles II, a job which paid so badly that she was jailed for debt. Her travels took her to Surinam (later Dutch Guiana) and the Netherlands. She wrote at least eighteen plays, much poetry and fifteen short novels.

Showing admirable flexibility, Behn reprinted 'To My Lady Morland at Tunbridge' eight years later, with only minor changes, under the title 'To Mrs Harsenet'.

The self-educated eldest child of a clergyman's family of fourteen, MARY MATILDA BETHAM (1776–1852) became quite a successful miniature painter. She finally overcame her scruples about appearing in print when she moved from Suffolk to London and published poetry, a *Biographical Dictionary of Celebrated Women* and the story of the minstrel Marie de France. Her family disliked her impoverished lifestyle, politics and religion; when she had a mental breakdown in the 1820s they had her committed to an asylum.

URSULA BETHELL (1874–1945) was born in England but grew up in New Zealand, where her father was a prosperous sheep farmer. After Swiss finishing schools and study at Oxford, she combined painting in Geneva and music in Dresden with working for charity. As a member of an Anglican community called the Grey Ladies she worked with London boys' clubs. Finally she settled in a cottage in the hills near Christchurch with Effie Pollen and began to publish her poetry.

'Discipline' and 'Fortune' were written for Effie Pollen in the third decade of their relationship.

Rumoured to be either Swiss or the illegitimate daughter of an Indian mother and an English father, ISA BLAGDEN (*c.* 1816–73) described her life as 'one long disappointment'. Little is known of her before 1849, when she made her home in Florence and became widely beloved among English expatriates, acting as a hostess and often nursing them. She was particularly close to Robert and ELIZABETH BARRETT BROWNING. She wrote novels, stories and articles, sometimes under the pseudonym 'Ivory Beryl', but her poems were not published till after her death. Her house in Florence was notoriously full of rescued dogs.

The daughter of a German Jewish banker, MATHILDE BLIND (1841–96) saw her life change course when her widowed mother married a revolutionary leader and the family fled to England in the early 1850s; Mathilde's brother later attempted to assassinate Bismarck. She was educated in London and Zurich, where she was not allowed entrance to university lectures; she went on a solo walk in the Swiss Alps at the age of nineteen and on her return became part of the Pre-Raphaelite circle. One of Blind's long poems was a protest against the brutal Highland clearances; another was inspired by Darwin; another was withdrawn by the publishers for its 'atheistic character'. Many of her later poems were inspired by her travels in Egypt and the Far East. She also wrote criticism on Shelley, several translations, short plays, two biographies and a novel. A suffragist, she left her entire estate to Newnham College, Cambridge, to found a women's scholarship in literature.

Born in Trinidad, DIONNE BRAND (b. 1953) moved to Toronto in 1970. She has taken degrees in English, philosophy, education and women's history. She has written fiction, including *Sans Souci and Other Stories* and her latest novel *In Another Place Not Here*. Her nonfiction works include a collection of oral histories, prose works on racism and video documentaries, but she is best known for her seven volumes of poetry.

The middle sister in the famous literary trio, EMILY BRONTË (1818–48) grew up in a Yorkshire parsonage and left the moors only for unhappy, homesick stints at boarding schools, at a *pension* in Brussels and in a brief teaching job near Halifax. Her father taught her to use pistols, but she was also known for her domestic efficiency. Emily was enraged when Charlotte read a private manuscript of her poetry in 1845, but the next year she agreed to go ahead with Charlotte and Anne in publishing a volume under the androgynous pseudonyms of Currer, Ellis and Acton Bell. Two years on, after the publication of her novel *Wuthering Heights*, Emily was taken ill at her brother's funeral and died of consumption, refusing all medical intervention, three months later.

BRENDA BROOKS (b. 1952) lives and writes in Toronto. Her first collection of poems, *Somebody Should Kiss You*, was published in 1990; *Blue Light in the Dash* followed in 1994.

OLGA BROUMAS (b. 1949) has published half a dozen volumes of poetry but is best known for her reworkings of myths and fairytales. In 1968 she moved from Syros, Greece, to the USA, where she studied architecture, taught English and women's studies and translated Greek literature, as well as working as a massage therapist and musician. Broumas is the founder of Freehand, Inc., a community of women artists. Recently she has been poet-in-residence at Brandeis University and has published several collaborative poems with T. Begley.

Eldest of twelve children of a physician whose money came from his Jamaican slave plantations, ELIZABETH BARRETT BROWNING (1806–61) grew up in Herefordshire, learning Greek and Latin from her brother's tutor and teaching herself Hebrew for good measure. Her mother encouraged her poetry, which Elizabeth published in volumes from the age of fourteen. After an adolescent illness or breakdown she became a semi-invalid, living in seclusion in her father's house in London, corresponding constantly with such friends as MARY RUSSELL MITFORD (who gave her a spaniel called Flush, later commemorated in a biography by Virginia Woolf). Her father forbade any of his children to marry; Elizabeth obeyed him till the age of forty, when she eloped with the poet Robert Browning and settled in Italy, where her private income supported them both. There she bore a son after several miscarriages, became interested in Italian Republican politics and spiritualism and wrote the feminist verse novel *Aurora Leigh*.

During her long invalidity Barrett Browning was fascinated and cheered by the works of the rather scandalous French novelist 'George Sand' (1804–76). They were not to meet till 1852 in Paris; Browning reported being overwhelmed with joy when Sand kissed her on the lips.

DOROTHEA PRIMROSE CAMPBELL (1793–1863) grew up in the Shetland Islands in a family crippled by debt, which she fought by publishing her poems by subscription. For some years she ran a school at Lerwick, despite ongoing illness and her mother's opium addiction; Walter Scott offered his support. She published a novel, getting twenty copies as her fee, then went to work for a family in England, who promptly went bankrupt. Campbell died at the Aged Governess's Asylum in London.

'To Miss Sophia Headle' is one of a group of poems addressed to the lost friends of Campbell's youth.

ALICE CARY (1820–71) grew up in a family of nine on a poor farm in Ohio, with little formal education. She and her sister Phoebe were publishing poems and hymns from their teens; in 1850 the proceeds from their first joint collection enabled them to move to New York City, where Alice led a sort of literary salon and Phoebe nursed her and ran the household. They both published poetry volumes individually, and Alice wrote much fiction about women's lives in farming communities. Both were suffragists and abolitionists; Alice was president of the first American women's club, Sorosis. The sisters died within six months of each other.

JANE CHAMBERS (1938–83) wrote two novels (one, *Burning*, about the Salem witches), several TV plays and twelve works for the stage, of which the best known is the widely toured *Last Summer at Bluefish Cove* (1980). Her single book of poetry, published after her death from brain cancer, is *Warrior at Rest*.

CHERYL CLARKE (b. 1947) writes highly sexual verse 'in the tradition of black women' as the subtitle of the first of her four collections puts it, often echoing the rhythms of jazz and blues. For ten years she was an editor of the lesbian–feminist magazine *Conditions*; she now directs the Office of Diverse Community Affairs and Lesbian–Gay Concerns at Rutgers University.

Daughter of an MP and a London heiress, CAROLINE CLIVE (1801–73) contracted paralysis at the age of three, and was left permanently lame. On her travels she caused scandal by visiting a hypnotist, going to the theatre alone and dining with her maid. Under the economical pseudonym of 'V' she published several volumes of verse, religious essays, satire on the Oxford Movement, a joint diary with her husband and sensational novels including *Paul Ferroll* (1855), notorious for its wicked hero. She also made detailed notes on her first pregnancy, which her 1940s editor suppressed as 'too indelicate' to publish. At sixty-four she was paralysed by a stroke and died eight years later in her library when her dress caught fire.

'The Mosel' is about the novelist Catherine Gore (1799–1861), with whom Caroline toured northern France in 1838 and for whom she felt 'nearly the strongest of my passions'.

ELIZA COBBE: *see* TUITE

A great-great-niece of the poet Samuel Taylor Coleridge, MARY COLERIDGE (1861–1907) was educated at home by a poet friend of her father who had lost his job as classics master at Eton after writing a love letter to a pupil. Another family friend, FANNY KEMBLE, was irritated when Mary was too shy to show any of her poetry and told her that such modesty bordered on 'self-love'. Coleridge taught at the Working Women's College in London, living all her life with her parents and sister, except for trips abroad with a group of close women friends known as the Quintette. Her reputation was based on a series of novels. For the publication of a handful of her poems (with which she was helped by Robert Bridges, father of ELIZABETH DARYUSH) she called herself 'Anodos' (Greek for 'the wanderer'). Over 200 more poems appeared after she died from acute appendicitis.

'The Witch' recalls *Christabel* (1816), an unfinished poem by Samuel Taylor Coleridge, in which Christabel rescues the beautiful stranger, Geraldine, who shares her bed and bewitches her in the night.

'Marriage' echoes some of Sappho's celebratory yet regretful wedding-songs for her pupils.

'Gone' is thought to be about the poet's older cousin Mildred Coleridge, whose friendship Mary was forced by her family to drop when Mildred made what they saw as an unsuitable marriage.

The reputation of FLORENCE CONVERSE (1871–1967) rests on her strikingly feminist novel, *Diana Victrix* (1897). She was assistant editor on the *Atlantic Monthly* for twenty-two years. Converse published other novels on historical and mythological themes, miracle plays and stories for children, a history of Wellesley College, Massachusetts, and poetry which was collected in 1937.

This pair of sonnets on 'Friendship' comes from a volume dedicated to Vida Scudder (1861–1954), a Wellesley professor (like KATHARINE LEE BATES and SOPHIE JEWETT), who worked to bring libraries and trade unions into the tenements. From 1919 Converse, Scudder and their mothers lived together, sharing 'both jokes and prayers'.

Daughter of the Poet Laureate Robert Bridges, ELIZABETH DARYUSH (1887–1977) grew up in rural Berkshire. She suppressed her first three volumes of poetry after publication; her later collections show a strong interest in metrical experimentation. Daryush spent four years in Persia (now Iran) in the 1920s and translated thirteenth-century mystic Sufi poetry. She returned to live near Oxford and her father.

One of the most famous society hostesses of her day, GEORGIANA SPENCER, DUCHESS OF DEVONSHIRE (1757–1806) set a fashion for wearing long feathers in the hair. She wrote poetry, letters and a novel, campaigned for the Whigs and enjoyed a scandalous but happy *ménage à trois* with her husband the Duke and Elizabeth Foster. Georgiana bore children (discreetly, on the Continent) to other men, including the future Prime Minister, Charles Grey, while running up gambling debts of over £100,000. Elizabeth gave the Duke several children before marrying him after Georgiana's death.

'To Lady Elizabeth Foster' was written when Georgiana was on the point of going blind.

EMILY DICKINSON (1830–86) was born, educated, lived and died in Amherst, Massachusetts. The daughter of a Congressman, she became increasingly reclusive, reading widely, corresponding with friends and writing several hundred poems a year; nearly 1,800 survive. She sent many to friends – HELEN HUNT JACKSON urged her to publish – and some to the editor T. W. Higginson, who advised toning down her idiosyncratic grammar and rhyme. One important figure in Dickinson's work is Sue Gilbert, who in 1856 married Emily's brother Austin and lived next door. Dickinson sent her a total of 276 poems over the years of their difficult relationship. Her poetry did not reach print till after her death, and a full edition came only in 1955.

The first verse of '"Heaven" – is what I cannot reach!' echoes a Sappho fragment about the highest apple on a tree, ripening unnoticed by the harvesters, or out of their reach.

H. D. (HILDA DOOLITTLE) (1886–1961) was brought up in Pennsylvania by a Moravian Protestant artist mother and an esoteric astronomer father. After a degree at Bryn Mawr, she moved to London, where Ezra Pound chose her pseudonym and promoted her 'Imagist' poetry. She edited *The Egoist* with T. S. Eliot, gave birth to a daughter, Perdita, and experimented with film-making, autobiography and fiction, but most of her fame rests on her poetry. Sigmund Freud, who psychoanalysed her in 1933, was a strong influence.

'At Baia' is thought to be about the writer Bryher (Annie Winnifred Ellerman, 1894–1983), who from 1919 supported H. D. financially, artistically and emotionally and helped her raise Perdita.

'Fragment Thirty-Six' is a reworking of one of the fragments of Sappho's work that had recently been discovered.

Born and raised in County Dublin, Ireland, MARY DORCEY (b. 1950) was one of the founders of Irishwomen United and the Irish Gay Rights Movement. She has lived in England, France, Japan and America, working as everything from waitress to disc-jockey, caterer to English-language teacher. Her poetry has been gathered in *Moving into the Space Cleared by Our Mothers* (1991) and her stories in *A Noise from the Woodshed* (1989).

CAROL ANN DUFFY (b. 1955) was born in Glasgow and brought up in Staffordshire. Her prizes have included the National Poetry Competition, the Somerset Maugham Award, the Dylan Thomas Award and the Scottish Arts Council Book Award of Merit. She is best known for dramatic monologues on controversial themes. As well as several volumes of poetry, she has had plays produced on stage and radio.

MAUREEN DUFFY (b. 1933) took a BA at King's College, London, and worked as a schoolteacher, becoming a full-time writer in 1962. She helped found the Writers' Action Group and has headed the Writers' Guild of Great Britain. Duffy has written poetry, plays (*Rites*, 1969, was set in a public toilet), an animal-rights handbook and biographies of Henry Purcell and APHRA BEHN, but she is best known for her novels. *The Microcosm* began as a documentary book about the lesbian underworld of the 1960s; *Gor Saga* was made into a TV film.

SUSANNA HIGHMORE DUNCOMBE (1725–1812), whose mother was a poet and father a painter, inherited both skills and displayed them as a member of the novelist Samuel Richardson's genteel artistic circle. She lived in Canterbury and had four children; only one daughter survived infancy and lived on with her mother, who in widowhood became notorious for keeping cats.

'To Aspasia', written before Susanna's marriage to John Duncombe, is a reply to a poem called 'To Stella' by Hester Mulso (later Chapone), inviting her to dedicate her life to female friendship.

'VIOLET FANE' (MARY MONTGOMERIE LAMB SINGLETON CURRIE) (1843–1905) wrote from an early age but used a pseudonym to hide it from her parents. She entered London high society with her first husband, an Irish landowner, and went to Constantinople and Rome with her second, an ambassador. Fane published three novels, a translation of the Queen of Navarre's memoirs, essays and seven volumes of poetry.

Born in Brooklyn, New York, MARGARETTA FAUGERES (1771–1801) was the daughter of the poet Ann Bleecker; she published their works together after her mother's death. Other publications include a tragedy in blank verse and a poem against capital punishment. Widowed at twenty-seven, Faugeres scraped a living for herself and her daughter by teaching.

'MICHAEL FIELD' was the joint pseudonym chosen by KATHARINE BRADLEY (1846–1914) and her niece EDITH COOPER (1862–1913). They lived together on family money as 'poets and lovers evermore' for almost fifty years, describing themselves as 'closer married' than their friend Robert had been to his wife ELIZABETH BARRETT BROWNING. Classical scholars and linguists, they published many volumes of poetry and heroic tragedies, as well as a memorial to their dog, Whym Chow. They received book-cover designs and advice on décor from the artist couple Charles Ricketts and Charles Shannon and moved to Richmond so that 'the Poets' could be near their dear friends 'the Painters'.

'Atthis, my darling, thou did'st stray' and 'Nought to me! So I choose to say' are from *Long Ago* (1889), a volume inspired by Sappho's fragments.

'Beloved, now I love God first' was written when the poets converted to Catholicism in 1907.

'Lovers' was written by Bradley while Cooper had cancer; 'I am thy charge, thy care!' followed after Cooper's death. Bradley had kept her own cancer secret; she died of it eight months after Cooper, in 1914.

ANNIE FIELDS (1834–1915) was born and spent her life in Boston. During her marriage to a publisher, she took an active part in the business as well as becoming a celebrated hostess, with her own literary salon. Widowed at forty-seven, Fields then had a thirty-year 'Boston marriage' (female partnership) with the novelist Sarah Orne Jewett; their circle included LOUISE GUINEY. On their travels in Europe, Fields and Jewett met Tennyson, Dickens and CHRISTINA ROSSETTI. As well as editing the letters and writing the biographies of her friends, Fields published three volumes of her own poetry, literary reminiscences and a bestselling handbook on charity work, *How to Help the Poor*.

ANNE FINCH: *see* WINCHILSEA

MARGARET FULLER (1810–50) was one of the most famous feminists of the nineteenth century. Born in Massachusetts, she was given a traditional masculine education by her politician father before going to boarding school; when he died, she educated her brothers and sisters. Fuller was the first woman to study at Harvard. She worked as a schoolteacher, literary critic for the *New York Tribune* and translator. With Emerson she produced the Transcendentalist journal *Dial*; on her own she wrote criticism, a history of the Roman revolution and her most famous work, *Woman in the Nineteenth Century* (1845). While in Rome she became friends with ELIZABETH BARRETT BROWNING, married the Marchese d'Ossoli, and had a son. Fuller died in a shipwreck on her way back to New York.

'To A. H. B.' is one of several poems written for Fuller's friend Anna Hazard Barker but left unpublished. After the painter Samuel G. Ward switched his attentions from Fuller to Barker, and married her in 1840, Fuller remained close to them both.

ELSA GIDLOW (1898–1986) was born in Yorkshire, England; when she was six the family moved to a tiny village in Quebec. Gidlow never went to school but worked on the railroads as her father's secretary before forming a literary group, publishing a magazine and studying at McGill. In the 1920s she moved to the California Bay Area and published the first of her openly lesbian poetry collections, *On a Grey Thread* (1923), being 'too ignorant and too courageous to know better'; the same confident spirit informs her autobiography. She founded the Society for Comparative Philosophy and her own publishing house, Druid Heights Books.

ROSA MULHOLLAND, LADY GILBERT (1841–1921) was the daughter of a Belfast doctor. She published much fiction aimed at young women as well as stories and poetry for children. Many of her novels raised public awareness of the 'Irish problem', and one prompted reform of the workhouses. *The Tragedy of Chris* (1903), in which a Dublin flower-seller follows her beloved partner who has been kidnapped for prostitution in London, is one of the last unselfconscious novels of romantic friendship.

Born into the Anglo-Irish aristocracy and celebrated by W. B. Yeats as a beautiful 'gazelle', EVA GORE-BOOTH (1870–1926) gave it all up to work for women workers' rights in Manchester with Esther Roper (1868–1938). Eva's sister Constance Markievicz fought for Ireland in 1916 and was elected the first woman Member of Parliament; by contrast, Eva and Esther were pacifists. In 1913 they moved to London for Eva's health and worked for the Women's Peace Crusade, the suffrage, and against capital punishment. Gore-Booth published prose, a study of St John's Gospel, and plays on Celtic themes but, above all, poetry.

In 'The Vision of Niamh', Gore-Booth imagines the legendary Irish warrior queen Maeve, shattered by the death of her daughter Fionavar, being consoled by love for Niamh, the goddess of spiritual beauty (an equivalent to Urania).

'The Travellers' is one of the few poems Gore-Booth wrote about the thirty years she spent with Esther Roper after their first meeting in Italy in 1896 at the house of the writer George MacDonald.

JUDY GRAHN (b. 1940) is the daughter of a cook and a photographer's assistant. After being expelled from the Air Force at twenty-one, she went on to become an activist, professor, publisher (founding the first all-women's press) and groundbreaking writer and cultural theorist. *Another Mother Tongue* (1984) mixes autobiography and queer cultural history; *The Highest Apple* (1985) discusses two centuries of a Sapphic poetic tradition; *Blood, Bread and Roses* (1993) is a theory of menstruation as the basis of culture. She has also published a fantasy novel, essays on GERTRUDE STEIN and poetry cycles based on the Tarot. Grahn is probably best known for her 'Common Woman' poems of 1971, which grittily celebrate the most marginal of working-class lives.

'Ah, Love, you smell of petroleum' is from a sequence called 'Confrontations with the Devil in the Form of Love'.

ANNE GRANT (1755–1838) was born in Glasgow but grew up in Albany, New York, where her father was an army officer. On marriage to a clergyman she returned to Scotland and settled in the remote Highland parish of Laggan, where she reared twelve children to speak Gaelic; only one of them survived her. She published an autobiography, an anti-feminist rebuttal to Mary Wollstonecraft, essays on local superstitions, an advice book for factory workers and much verse, including 'Where and O where is your Highland laddie gone?', but she was most famous for her books of letters. For her last eighteen years of widowhood she walked on crutches but enjoyed an active literary life in Edinburgh.

'The Nymph of the Fountain to Charlotte' is one of several poems to a relation of hers who died a few years later while giving birth to her first child.

DORA GREENWELL (1821–82), the daughter of the Deputy Lieutenant of Lancaster, taught herself languages, political economy and philosophy. She published poetry (often religious) and helped Josephine Butler in her campaign against the hounding of prostitutes under the Contagious Diseases Acts. Other social work included essays on the education of 'idiots and imbeciles' and defences of the anti-vivisection league, as well as women's right to education, work and the vote. When she settled in Durham with her invalid mother in 1854, Greenwell's literary friends included CHRISTINA ROSSETTI. In 1871 her mother's death freed her to move; she lived mainly in London, and became addicted to opium.

Greenwell met ELIZABETH BARRETT BROWNING only once, but her fervent admiration for her is clear from these two sonnets.

Born in Massachusetts to a white mother who soon left and a lawyer father, the son of a slave, ANGELINA WELD GRIMKÉ (1880–1958) was publishing poems by the age of thirteen, though never any of her love poems to women. Her great-aunts, whom she found inspiring, were the essayists and abolitionists Angelina Emily Grimké and Sarah Moore Grimké. Angelina Weld Grimké also produced short stories and a play about racism but seems to have stopped writing after her father's death in 1930.

Daughter of an Irish-American Civil War brigadier-general, LOUISE GUINEY (1861–1920) was educated in New England convents. To support herself and her widowed mother, Guiney published collections of poetry, essays, fiction, biographies of Robert Emmett and Blessed Edmund Campion, a selected edition of the works of KATHERINE PHILIPS, a fifteenth-century French romance and an anthology of Roman Catholic poets. She was a member of the Boston literary circle around Sarah Orne Jewett and ANNIE FIELDS. Having been forced out of her job as a postmistress (probably due to her sex and religion), Guiney suffered two nervous breakdowns before taking a job as a librarian. After many literary tours of England, she made herself a second home in Oxford. 'Private Theatricals', from her first volume, is quite untypical of Guiney's poetry, which tends towards the stirring and the mystical.

MARILYN HACKER (b. 1942), a New Yorker from the Bronx, has been a teacher, an antiquarian bookseller and the editor of a science-fiction quarterly and several feminist literary magazines, as well as raising a daughter. Her poetry veers from English to French, from formal strictness to bawdy slang; the prizes it has won include the Lambda Literary Award and the National Book Award.

'Coming Downtown' is a villanelle from *Love, Death and the Changing of the Seasons* (1986), a novel in traditional verse forms which tells of the year-long passion between an older and a younger woman.

ELIZABETH HANDS (late eighteenth century), 'born in obscurity' as she put it, was for many years a domestic servant near Coventry. Her marriage to a blacksmith seems to have allowed her to give more time to her poetry; her longest work, *The Death of Amnon* (1789), is a biblical epic about incestuous rape.

'An Epistle' can be read as a perfect example of romantic friendship poetry or possibly (as Donna Landry has suggested) as a servant's parody of such upper-class affectation.

GILLIAN HANSCOMBE (b. 1945), from Melbourne, has raised a son, written about lesbian motherhood, modernist women writers and Dorothy Richardson. She is the author of the classic feminist epistolary novel *Between Friends* (1982). Her latest work of fiction, *Figments of a Murder* (1995), is concerned with ethics and the meaning of murder within the feminist community. Her most recent lyric sequence is 'The Interloper' in *Conservations of Love* (1996). She lives and writes in Devon with SUNITI NAMJOSHI.

'Well, then let slip the masks' is from *Flesh and Paper*, a volume of poems that grew out of the long-distance correspondence through which the poets fell in love after meeting at a conference in London in 1984.

Born with a heart condition, LESBIA HARFORD (1891–1927) none the less graduated in law and worked in textile factories, becoming a radical labour activist in the International Workers of the World, known as the Wobblies. She published only a handful of poems in her lifetime, being, as she put it, 'in no hurry to be read'.

'I count the days' and 'I can't see the sunshine' are two of the many poems she wrote for her first and longest lover, Katie Lush (d. 1935), a philosophy tutor at Melbourne University, where they met.

EMILY HICKEY (1845–1924) grew up in a castle in Waterford, Ireland, where her father was the rector; it was the poetry of ELIZABETH BARRETT BROWNING that started Hickey writing in her teens. In her early twenties she went to London in search of fame, and lived with the Macmillans, the publishers. She worked as a secretary, private tutor and governess, was involved in the movement for women's higher education, became a lecturer at the North London Collegiate School for Girls, founded the (Robert) Browning Society and published volumes of poetry – one of which she destroyed later, when she was a High Church Anglican, because of a disrespectful line about Jesus. She suffered a nervous breakdown, then went blind, but continued writing on a typewriter for another two years before she died.

'For Richer, For Poorer' echoes the Marriage Service in its title, the

Gospel parable of the wise and foolish virgins in its first verse and the speech of Ruth to Naomi (from the Book of Ruth) in its last two lines.

'I Think of You as of a Good Life-boat' was published in a volume dedicated to Hickey's 'very dear friend Annie Eleanor Ridley [1871–1895]'.

Nothing is known about the parents of ANNIE HINDLE (*c.* 1847–after 1897), the most famous of the early male impersonators. Born in England, she was adopted by a Hertfordshire woman who gave the child her own name and put her to work singing in taverns. After success with a drag routine on the London stage, Hindle found fame and fortune in American vaudeville halls as a performer and (briefly) a manager. She was legally married twice: in 1868 to the English actor Charles Vivian, who battered her, and in 1886 (in costume) to her stage dresser, Annie Ryan. After her wife's death in their New Jersey home in 1891, Hindle seems to have gone back on the stage. She published a number of poems in the *New York Clipper* in the 1870s.

Daughter of a professor, HELEN HUNT JACKSON (1830–85) was raised by an aunt in Amherst, Massachusetts. She began to write only at the urging of T. W. Higginson after the death of her husband and two sons, and preferred to remain anonymous. She published (in a blood-red cover) an exposé of government maltreatment of native tribes, presenting a copy to every US Congressman; this helped to put a spark to the Indian Rights movement. Her novel *Ramona* was meant to do for Native Americans what her friend Harriet Beecher Stowe had done for African-Americans with *Uncle Tom's Cabin*; it went into 300 reprints. Jackson was a lifelong friend of EMILY DICKINSON.

Daughter of a New York country doctor, SOPHIE JEWETT (1861–1909) moved to Buffalo as a child. With her artist sister she travelled almost every summer, spending long periods in England and Italy. In 1890 Jewett became a professor of Anglo-Saxon at Wellesley College, Massachusetts; one colleague and friend was KATHARINE LEE BATES. Entirely self-educated, she published a translation of the medieval poem *The Pearl*, an edition of Tennyson's *The Holy Grail* and two collections of her own poetry.

JACKIE KAY (b. 1961) was born in Edinburgh, brought up in Glasgow and lives in London. Her first book of poems explored her experience of being a black child adopted by white parents. She has written several plays; *Twilight Shift* (1994) is about the love affair between a miner and a barber in a small Scottish mining community.

Born in London, FRANCES KEMBLE (1809–1903) was raised by a spinster aunt and schooled mainly in France. Her father Charles Kemble, trying to save his Covent Garden theatre from bankruptcy, persuaded Frances to make her début as Juliet in 1829, playing opposite both her parents; despite success in this and other seasons, she always found acting 'utterly distasteful'. After touring the USA, she married a Philadelphia plantation owner; he tried to stop her working for the abolition of slavery, and after eleven years she sailed back to England to get a divorce, losing custody of both her daughters. In the 1850s she became a close friend of ELIZABETH BARRETT BROWNING, who was amused by Kemble's rule of wearing all her clothes in strict rotation. Fanny supported herself by acting, giving Shakespearian reading tours and publishing poetry and reminiscences; at seventy-nine she produced her first novel.

   'Parting' seems to be one of the many poems Kemble wrote for Harriet St Leger over the course of their fifty-year correspondence, grieving that their love had to be 'transatlantic'.

Daughter to a royal chaplain, ANNE KILLIGREW (1660–85) was maid of honour (along with ANNE FINCH, COUNTESS OF WINCHILSEA) to the Duchess of York. Her poetry and paintings won high praise from such critics as John Dryden before smallpox killed her at the age of twenty-five.

   Killigrew's father included 'On the Soft and Gentle Motions of Eudora' with two other love poems to 'Eudora' as an appendix at the end of his daughter's posthumous collection but insisted that, though found among her papers, they were not her work. There is no evidence for his claim.

CHARLOTTE LENNOX (*c.* 1729–1804) was the daughter of an army officer but later claimed he had been Governor of New York. She came to live with an aunt in England who turned out to have gone mad. With the help of such mentors as Samuel Johnson, Lennox managed to scrape a living by writing everything from pastoral drama to a source study of Shakespeare. Her most famous novel is *The*

Female Quixote (1752). Lennox made enemies as easily as friends; a maid once took her to court for assault. After more than forty years of supporting her husband, Lennox separated from him and applied to the Royal Literary Fund for money to send her son to America, away from his 'most unnatural father'.

'Ardelia to Flavia, an Epistle' was probably written for Lennox's first literary patron, Lady Isabella Finch, with whom she often quarrelled before finally denouncing her in her novel *The Life of Harriot Stuart* (1750).

AMY LEVY (1861–89) grew up in Brighton, publishing her first poem in a feminist journal at thirteen. She was the first Jewish student at Newnham College, Cambridge; after four terms she returned to her parents' home in London. She travelled across Europe, then settled in a London garret, wrote for Oscar Wilde's *Women's World* and published a defence of Socrates' wife, three novels about the Jewish community and several collections of poetry, including a dramatic monologue about the suicide of 'A Minor Poet'. Though she mixed in London literary circles, her deafness and her fits of depression increasingly isolated her.

'London in July' and 'At a Dinner Party' were published in a volume dedicated to Levy's close friend and travelling companion, the writer, suffragist and socialist Clementina Black (1855–1923). A week after correcting the proofs, Levy killed herself at her parents' house by inhaling charcoal fumes.

DOROTHY LIVESAY (b. 1909) was born in Winnipeg, Manitoba, and went to university in California and Paris. Her father was the general manager of Canadian Press; her mother was a writer. Livesay has published more than a dozen volumes of poetry since 1928, winning the Queen's Canada and Governor General's Medals, as well as editing two anthologies of poems by women. She has worked as a journalist, schoolteacher, professor, social worker, editor and broadcaster (writing a documentary drama about Japanese–Canadians). She helped found the League of Canadian Poets and Amnesty International (Canada).

AUDRE LORDE (1934–92), born in New York to Caribbean parents, was one of the most influential of feminists. She studied at the National University of Mexico, Hunter College and Columbia University before becoming a librarian, professor, publisher (co-founding Kitchen Table:

Women of Color Press), poet-in-residence and mother to a son and daughter. Her works include five volumes of poetry, books of essays, speeches, an autobiographical fiction or 'biomythography' called *Zami* (1982), and *The Cancer Journals* about the disease she fought for more than a decade. She was New York State Poet Laureate from 1991 to 1993.

Born into a rich Massachusetts family, AMY LOWELL (1874–1925) published her first book of stories at the age of thirteen. Only after years of volunteer work, travel and socializing did she begin writing poetry in 1902. She travelled to England to form connections with other Imagists (H. D., Ezra Pound) and edited anthologies of Imagist (or, as Pound called it resentfully, 'Amygist') poetry. She was hugely fat except for her tiny feet, slept on mounds of pillows and smoked black cigars; her confident eccentricity irritated many contemporaries, but her critical works and poetry had to be taken seriously.

The poems included are from 'Two Speak Together', a sequence written ten years into Lowell's partnership with the actress Ada Russell.

The poet, novelist and religious writer CHARLOTTE MACCARTHY (mid eighteenth century) was the daughter of an Irish Protestant gentleman. By 1749 she was to be found selling theatre tickets in London. When her anti-Catholic book *Justice and Reason* (1757) met with opposition, MacCarthy insisted that the Jesuits were trying to poison her.

'Contentment, to a Friend' is one of the poems appended to her 1745 novel of romance, cross-dressing and female friendship, *The Fair Moralist*.

'To the Same' is the third in a sequence of poems addressed to 'Chloe' (real name unknown).

ISABEL ECCLESTONE MACKAY (1875–1928) was a prolific Canadian writer. She published poetry for adults and children, several plays and half a dozen novels, as well as a collection of West Coast Indian legends.

Daughter of the chairman of the Bank of New Zealand, KATHERINE MANSFIELD (1888–1923) studied at Queen's College, London, and learned secretarial skills at Wellington Technical College but was writing full-time by 1910. Though she wrote journals, letters and poetry, it was short stories for which she became famous, earning Virginia Woolf's friendship and envy. From 1918 Mansfield spent her winters in the south of France, fighting off the tuberculosis that was to kill her at thirty-five.

'Friendship', a poem from Mansfield's scrapbook, is about her companion for twenty troubled years, Ida Baker or 'LM'.

DAPHNE MARLATT (b. 1942) is a Vancouver poet and prose writer. She was a founding editor of the feminist magazine *Tessera* and has published two books of oral history as well as many volumes of poetry, some in collaboration with the poet Betsy Warland, who was her partner for eleven years.

'Coming to you' is part of a sequence, *Touch to My Tongue*, written for Betsy Warland.

MARY MASTERS (*c.* 1694–1771) was daughter to a poor Norwich schoolteacher who disapproved of intellectual ambition in women; none the less, she managed to gather enough rich acquaintances to subscribe to her first book of poetry. Later she lived with various London literary friends (Edward Cave, Elizabeth Carter, Catharine Macaulay) and published letters on love and the equality of the sexes.

'To the Same; Enquiring Why I Wept' follows another poem to 'Olinda' (real name unknown), who has fallen seriously ill after the poet's own recovery.

Piecing together the ill-fitting jigsaw that is the life of ADAH ISAACS MENKEN (*c.* 1839–68), it seems that she was born in New Orleans, had four or five husbands (some bigamously) and lost two sons in infancy. Though she wrote for American papers and gathered a collection of dramatic free verse which was published a week after her early death, she has gone down in the history books only for appearing in *Mazeppa*, a play based on a Byron poem, in which she crossed the stage almost nude, tied to a horse.

CHARLOTTE MEW (1869–1928) spent her life in Bloomsbury, London, apart from holidays in France and the Isle of Wight. Her family was dogged by childhood death and mental illness. Mew supplemented the family finances by writing essays, stories and poems for magazines. She also worked with Miss Paget's Girls' Club and visited widows on behalf of the War Pensions Committee. After the publication of Mew's first volume of poetry at forty-seven, Thomas Hardy and Virginia Woolf called her the greatest living woman poet, but Mew continued to destroy most of her manuscripts, sometimes setting them on fire to light her cigarettes. Four foot ten, always in a long tweed coat, she was seen as a brilliant eccentric. The flow of poems slowed to a trickle as first her mother, then her only surviving sister Anne died after long illnesses. Depressed by poverty, convinced that Anne had been buried alive and afraid of hereditary insanity, while in a nursing home Mew killed herself by drinking disinfectant.

The reference to Paris seems to link 'Rooms' to Mew's frustrated love for Ella D'Arcy, whom she pursued to Paris in 1902.

EDNA ST VINCENT MILLAY (1892–1950) was brought up by her mother in Maine after her parents divorced. On graduating from Vassar she directed her own plays for the Provincetown Players in Greenwich Village, New York, but relied for an income on magazine sketches written under a pseudonym. Her volumes of frank love poetry were a huge success in the 1920s; after two years in Europe as a *Vanity Fair* correspondent, she became the first woman to win the Pulitzer Prize for poetry.

MARY RUSSELL MITFORD (1786–1855) spent her life with her parents near Reading. Her adored father was a gambler who kept reducing the family to poverty from which only Mary's publications saved them. Her first love was poetry, but plays and sketches of village life paid better; by the end of her career she was resorting to the writing of almanacs and anthologies to support her parents. What kept her sane was her extensive network of correspondents, including her closest friend, ELIZABETH BARRETT BROWNING; her letters are her most enduring legacy.

As a child, MARY MOLLINEUX (*c.* 1651–95) had weak eyes that prevented her from sewing; this proved a godsend, as her father taught her Latin, Greek, mathematics and surgery instead. Though she had enough nerve to debate with bishops and serve jail terms as a Quaker, Mollineux felt 'not free' to seek praise by publishing her religious poetry in her lifetime, but the Quakers made her name by publishing a posthumous collection with a preface by her cousin Frances Owen.

'Another Letter to a Friend' is one of a number of poems Mollineux wrote to a woman known only as F. R. – possibly the initials of Frances Owen before marriage.

ELIZABETH MOODY (d. 1814) published occasional poems from around 1760. She got literary advice and support from the poet Edward Lovibond, reviewed fiction for the *Monthly Review* for ten years and published *Poetical Trifles* in London in 1798.

An actor's daughter born on a ship in the Irish Sea, SYDNEY OWENSON, LADY MORGAN (1776–1859) came to symbolize Romantic Ireland to the English. Literary fame raised her from governess to society hostess, and she was the first woman to receive a pension for 'services to the world of letters'. She published poems, patriotic sketches, ballads and historical novels that often attacked reactionary regimes, as well as a cross-cultural history, *Woman and Her Master.*

'Fragment III' was written for the novelist Alicia Lefanu, daughter of the novelist and playwright Frances Sheridan and sister of the playwright Richard Sheridan.

ROSA MULHOLLAND: *see* GILBERT

SUNITI NAMJOSHI (b. 1941) was educated in India, the USA and Canada. She worked in the Indian Administrative Service, then taught at the University of Toronto for many years. She is known as a fabulist and a poet. Her collaboration with her partner, GILLIAN HANSCOMBE, has produced some extraordinary work. The last chapter of her latest book, *Building Babel* (1996), has been put on the Internet by the publishers, and contributions are invited to the Babel Building Site at http://www.publishaust.net.au/~spinifex/buildingbabelsite.html.

'Well, then let slip the masks' is from *Flesh and Paper*, a volume of poems that grew out of the long-distance correspondence through which the poets fell in love after meeting at a conference in London in 1984.

Daughter of a London chemist, EDITH NESBIT (1858–1924) is best known for her children's fiction but also wrote poetry, journalism, plays and (when she needed the money) verses for greeting cards. Though she saw no need for the vote for women, she was politically radical, helping to found the Fabian Society, and lived a Bohemian life, raising a total of five children in a *ménage à trois.*

FRANCES OSGOOD (1811–50) was educated at home in Boston and published poetry from the age of fourteen. During two profitable years in England she produced two volumes of verse and a lyric drama. Back in New York, she edited the *Ladies' Companion*; her literary circle included Poe, Melville and Hawthorne. She died after a three-year struggle with tuberculosis.

SYDNEY OWENSON: *see* MORGAN

PAT PARKER (1944–89) was an African-American poet whose work was marked by her involvement in the civil rights, black liberation, feminist and gay liberation movements. Her solo and concert performances of her poetry were very popular; with JUDY GRAHN she released a recording, *Where Would I Be Without You*. She also ran the Oakland Feminist Women's Health Center and raised two daughters.

Born in Birmingham, BESSIE RAYNER PARKES (1829–1925) grew up in London and Warwickshire. She published three books of poetry before becoming one of the leading feminist activists of her age. With her friend Barbara Bodichon she ran the *English Women's Journal* in 1858 and formed a committee to draw up the petition for the Married Women's Property Bill. Brought up a Unitarian, she was agnostic for a time before converting to Catholicism in her thirties. After her marriage in 1867 she lived mainly in France. Her son was the poet Hilaire Belloc.

KATHERINE PHILIPS (1631–64), the daughter of a London merchant, settled in Wales on her marriage to a kindly man thirty-eight years her senior. She became known as the 'Matchless Orinda' for her poetry which was read in manuscript with much admiration by the women and men in her 'Society of Friendship'. By the time of her death she had produced an important body of work, but a collected edition did not appear until 1990.

'To Mrs M. A. Upon Absence' is about Mary Aubrey or 'Rosania', who was Philips's first love; they met at boarding-school in London in the early 1640s.

'To Rosania (now Mrs Mountague) being with her, 25th September 1652' seems to concern a frustrating visit to Mary Aubrey Mountague after her marriage. They remained close, however, and it was Mary who nursed Katherine when she died from smallpox in her early thirties.

'To My Excellent Lucasia, On Our Friendship' is about Anne Owen (the successor to Rosania), named 'Lucasia' on her admission to the 'Society of Friendship' in December 1651. When Owen in turn got married, Philips went to Ireland for a year to be with her.

MARJORIE PICKTHALL (1883–1922) was born in Middlesex, England, but her family moved to Toronto when she was six; she spent her life between the two countries. She worked as a librarian and (during the First World War) an ambulance driver and farmer. Her publications include novels for adults and children, often focusing on Canadian life in the pioneer days, and verse drama as well as poetry.

RUTH PITTER (1897–1992) grew up in London but formed her attachment to nature during holidays in a primitive cottage her schoolteacher parents rented in Epping Forest. During the First World War she worked as a War Office clerk (becoming so underfed and miserable that she had seventeen boils on her body), then found greater happiness as a furniture-maker. From 1930 she ran a craft workshop in Chelsea with her companion, Kathleen O'Hara. In 1920 began a stream of volumes of formally traditional poems, for which Pitter was the first woman to receive the Queen's Gold Medal for poetry; she also published 'grotesques' on gardening and cats. Her friends included DOROTHY WELLESLEY. When the Second World War put paid to the craft workshop, Pitter turned to journalism and broadcasting, appearing weekly on the BBC's *Brains Trust*.

Orphaned young, SARAH PONSONBY (1755–1831) grew up with distant relations in Kilkenny, Ireland, where at the age of thirteen she met the twenty-nine-year-old Eleanor Butler. Thwarting the best efforts of their families to marry Sarah off and put Eleanor in a convent, they 'eloped' (as one relation put it) to North Wales in 1778. Over the course of the half century they spent in impoverished but blissful domesticity, the 'Ladies of Llangollen' became the most famous example of romantic friendship.

'Song' was written in the Day Book kept by Sarah during her thirteenth year with her 'Beloved' in Llangollen Vale.

Born and raised in Alabama, MINNIE BRUCE PRATT (b. 1946) moved in 1982 to Washington, DC, where she helped found a lesbian–feminist action group, LIPS, and was on the collective of *Feminary*. She has run workshops and published essays on racism and anti-Semitism. Pratt's award-winning second volume of poetry, *Crimes Against Nature* (1990), was nominated for the Pulitzer Prize; it was inspired by losing her two sons to her ex-husband when he discovered she was a lesbian. Her stories, *S/He*, explore the experience of having a transgendered lover.

LIZETTE WOODWORTH REESE (1856–1935) was a teacher of English literature for almost half a century. She published nine volumes of poetry as well as volumes of reminiscences about growing up in Maryland and an autobiographical novel.

'Nocturne' and 'To a Dead Friend' are two of several elegies published in a collection dedicated to the memory of Laura V. de Valin and Anne Cullington.

Born in the Bronx, NAOMI REPLANSKY (b. 1918) has spent her life in New York, apart from a few years in France. She has worked as a lathe operator, computer programmer and teacher. Collections of her poetry appeared in 1952 (*Ring Song*, nominated for the National Book Award), 1988 and 1994. She has also translated German and Yiddish literature.

ADRIENNE RICH (b. 1929). Since the selection of her first volume by W. H. Auden for the Yale Series of Younger Poets in 1951, Rich's work has continually broken new ground, moving from closed forms to a feminist poetics and a radical urban imagination and politics. Her books include *Collected Early Poems 1950–1970*, *The Dream of a Common Language*, *Your Native Land, Your Life*, *An Atlas of the Difficult World*, *Dark Fields of the Republic* and, in prose, *Of Woman Born*, *On Lies, Secrets and Silence*, *Blood, Bread and Poetry* and *What is Found There: Notebooks on Poetry and Politics*. Her work has received many awards including the Ruth Lilly Prize, the Poets' Prize, the Lambda Literary Award, the Lenore Marshall/Nation Award, and a MacArthur Fellowship.

MICHELE ROBERTS (b. 1949), born in Hertfordshire to a French mother and English father, was educated at Oxford before working as a librarian, cook, typist, cleaner, pregnancy aid counsellor, and editor for *Spare Rib* and *City Limits*. She has published three collections of poetry and eight novels, as well as short stories and plays. She is a regular reviewer and broadcaster. Her novel *Daughters of the House* was shortlisted for the Booker Prize in 1992 and won the W. H. Smith Literary Award in 1993.

'Magnificat' uses a pattern of imagery from the first chapter of the

Gospel of Luke. The Annunciation refers to the Angel Gabriel's appearance to Mary to tell her she will give birth to Jesus; the Visitation is Mary's visit to her cousin Elizabeth when both are pregnant; the Magnificat is a prayer based on Mary's speech about God's goodness.

ELIZA ROBERTSON (1771–1805) left her London home at the age of fifteen to begin teaching; her father helped her to set up her first school, but his debts sank it. She published stories, a grammar and sermons for children. From 1795 she and Miss Charlotte Sharp ran another school at Greenwich; having inherited some money, Robertson tried to improve the school building, fell into debt again and seems to have been jailed and accused of being a prostitute, a man in disguise or a lover of women. She defended herself in a variety of autobiographical treatises, verses and fiction.

'A Poetical Epistle to an Absent Friend' was written from Huntingdon jail in 1801. Despite all the hopes of pastoral domesticity expressed in this poem, Robertson and Sharp fell out bitterly the following year and attacked each other in print.

A. MARY F. ROBINSON (1857–1944) was educated in Coventry (where her father was employed as an architect), Brussels, Italy and London, specializing in Greek literature. As well as publishing volumes of poetry and a novel, she wrote about Charlotte and EMILY BRONTË and Robert and ELIZABETH BARRETT BROWNING. Based in France for many years, Robinson ran a Paris salon, wrote in both languages and aimed to strengthen Anglo-French literary relations. Her beloved sister was the novelist Frances Mabel Robinson.

'Rosa Rosarum' may have been written for Robinson's lover, the critic 'Vernon Lee' (Violet Paget), to whom she addressed the poems collected in *A Handful of Honeysuckle* (1878).

Sister to the painter and poet Dante Gabriel Rossetti, CHRISTINA ROSSETTI (1830–94) wrote over 900 poems in English and sixty in Italian. During a troubled adolescence she ripped her arm with a pair of scissors in a rage against her mother, and at one point mortified herself by giving up all pleasures, such as chess and theatre. Her grandfather had her first volume of poetry privately printed when she was seventeen; she went on to publish children's verse, short stories and volumes that mixed poetry and prose. She applied to join Florence Nightingale in the Crimea but was rejected as too young; instead she worked in a Home for Fallen Women (ex-prostitutes) and lived at home with her mother. Rossetti was a fervent High Anglican and claimed to have rejected both her suitors on the grounds of their religious indecisiveness. For more than twenty years she suffered from Graves' disease, a disfigurement which made her even more socially reclusive; she finally died two years after an operation for breast cancer.

Daughter to a Dissenting Presbyterian minister, ELIZABETH SINGER ROWE (1674–1737) started publishing poetry in her twenties and found rich patrons; one of her friends was ANNE FINCH, COUNTESS OF WINCHILSEA. Widowed at forty-one, Rowe settled down to a life of pious seclusion in Somerset, where she educated local children and wrote religious fiction. She was influential long after her death as a virtuous role model for women writers.

'To Cleone' uses the technique of Rowe's bestselling collection of 'letters from the dead to the living', *Friendship in Death* (1728).

VITA SACKVILLE-WEST (1892–1962) is better known for her garden, love-affairs, 'lavender marriage' and fictional incarnation as the hero(ine) of Virginia Woolf's *Orlando* (1928) than for her own works. Born at Knole in Kent, the largest private house in England, but barred by her sex from inheriting it, Sackville-West wrote about Knole in histories as well as novels. She also produced gardening columns, travel books and many biographies (of, for instance, St Joan, her grandmother and APHRA BEHN). Her poetry tends to use traditional forms to celebrate women and the land.

'No Obligation' dates from 1932, when Sackville-West was involved in a complex sexual triangle with Evelyn Irons and Olive Rinder.

Born in Belgium, MAY SARTON (1912–95) grew up in Massachusetts. She founded the Apprentice Theatre to perform neglected European plays, then held down a series of teaching jobs; from one of these she was fired for publishing the openly lesbian novel *Mrs. Stevens Hears the Mermaids Singing* (1974). She alternated novels with poetry but also produced documentary film scripts, plays, translations from French poetry, memoirs and diaries exploring her solitude and old age in Maine; her works total fifty-four volumes.

ANTOINETTE SCUDDER (1898–after 1949) was an American writer who published two dozen plays on historical and mythological themes, as well as many volumes of poetry, collected in 1947.

Known as the 'Swan of Lichfield' after the town where her poet father was canon, ANNA SEWARD (1742–1809) claimed to have read Milton from the age of two. Though she was lamed by an accident and stayed at home to look after her father, Seward enjoyed corresponding with other writers and won fame for her literary opinions as well as her poetry. She was devoted to Eleanor Butler and SARAH PONSONBY, the 'Ladies of Llangollen'; she wrote a poem praying that they might die together, when the time came, under a single bolt of lightning.

Sonnet X and Sonnet XXXI are from a long sequence Seward began before the marriage of her beloved adoptive sister Honora Sneyd to Richard Edgeworth (father of the novelist Maria Edgeworth), which destroyed their friendship in 1773. Honora died of consumption in 1780; in the second sonnet Seward accuses Richard Edgeworth of a callous visit to the theatre on the night of the death.

Born in Inverness, ALI SMITH (b. 1962) studied at Aberdeen and Cambridge. She has worked as a sandwich packer, cinema usher and university lecturer. As well as poetry and several plays, she has published a collection of short stories, *Free Love* (1995), and a novel, *Like* (forthcoming, 1997).

GEORGIANA SPENCER: *see* DEVONSHIRE

GERTRUDE STEIN (1874–1946) was born in Pennsylvania to Jewish parents who were in business. She studied medicine but failed her final exams, claiming to be bored. Two years later she settled in Paris with her brother Leo, buying paintings and running a Saturday-night salon for expatriates and avant-garde artists; apart from lecture tours of the States, she was to stay in France for the rest of her life. Her writing (in a range of genres that includes, but is by no means limited to, family chronicle, autobiography, lecture, children's story, portrait, play, opera and poem) defies description.

The second section of the long poem *Lifting Belly* is set in Mallorca where Stein and Alice B. Toklas, her partner in all things from 1910, spent some of the First World War.

ALICE V. STUART (1899–1983) was born in Rangoon, Burma, of Scottish parents; her father was a writer. She was educated at St Hilda's School in Edinburgh and Somerville College, Oxford. She worked as a tutor to foreign students, organized poetry recitals, helped found the Scottish Association for the Speaking of Verse, and published several volumes of poetry. Some of her poems are in Scots dialect, others are on religious themes, and many are addressed to the dead.

MAY SWENSON (1913–89) was born and raised in Utah but spent most of her life in New York. At intervals in her writing career she worked as a reporter, secretary, ghost writer and editor. She was a chancellor of the American Academy of Poets and published eleven volumes of poetry.

'Poet to Tiger' is one of a group of poems dedicated to her partner, the novelist Rozanne R. Knudson.

SARA TEASDALE (1884–1933) grew up in St Louis, Missouri, the daughter of a food wholesaler. She and her friends produced a manuscript magazine in which her first poems appeared. From 1916 she lived in New York, producing critically acclaimed volumes of poetry every few years; one influential friend was AMY LOWELL. Depressed by ill health and the suicide of the poet Vachel Lindsay, Teasdale died of an overdose before she could complete her biography of CHRISTINA ROSSETTI.

'Song' was written for Marion Stanley when she took Teasdale on a desperately needed holiday to Arizona.

ELIZABETH TEFT (1723–after 1747) grew up in Lincoln and is known only for her poetry collection *Orinthia's Miscellanies* (1747), which touches on marriage, religion, a visit to Bedlam and the Jacobite rebellion.

EDITH THOMAS (1854–1925) grew up in Ohio before her uncle introduced her to New York, where she made her home for the rest of her life. HELEN HUNT JACKSON helped her to start publishing poems in magazines in 1881. A year after her death Thomas's *Selected Poems* appeared with a memoir based on materials supplied by her 'life-long friend', Miss Charlotte Bingham.

Though her father had been an eminent London lawyer, ELIZABETH THOMAS (1675–1731) struggled with poverty all her life and on one occasion went to jail for debt. Dryden encouraged her poetry, but Pope (angered by her sale of some of his letters) destroyed her reputation in his *Dunciad* (1728). She also wrote autobiography and letters, particularly to Richard Gwinnett, in a sixteen-year courtship ended by his death.

'To Clemena' is one of several poems to Thomas's cousin, Anne Osborne.

Born in County Dublin, Ireland, ELIZA COBBE, LADY TUITE (1764–1850) published prose for children as well as poetry on patriotic and friendship themes. By 1796 she seems to have been living in Bath in bad health and with so little money that she had to write to her baroness aunt for help.

THELMA TYFIELD (1906–68) studied at the University of Cape Town and worked as an English teacher. From 1943 to 1961 she was headmistress of the Good Hope Seminary Girls' High School. She published a popular English grammar book and two anthologies of English poetry. Her own poems were collected, after her death, in *Time Prized* (1972).

Born in Middlesex, England, SYLVIA TOWNSEND WARNER (1893–1978) worked in a munitions factory and edited an encyclopaedia of Tudor church music before meeting VALENTINE ACKLAND, going to the Spanish Civil War and settling in Dorset. Townsend Warner is not as well known for her half-dozen poetry collections as for her novels, the subjects of which range from witches, to medieval nuns, to the Paris revolution of 1848.

The poems included are from a joint collection of 1934, *Whether a Dove or a Seagull*.

DOROTHY WELLESLEY, DUCHESS OF WELLINGTON (1889–1956) was educated at home and wrote poetry from an early age, producing ten volumes in all while raising two children. Addicted to travel, Wellesley spent the First World War in Italy, travelled to Persia (now Iran) and Russia with VITA SACKVILLE-WEST and made a series of journeys to the East with Hilda Matheson. She sponsored and edited the first Hogarth Press Living Poets series and, with W. B. Yeats, edited the Cuala Press broadsides.

HELEN HAY WHITNEY (1875–1944) published poetry for adults and children, as well as romances.

This sonnet is from a long sequence addressing a woman, contrasting this tormenting passion with the speaker's calm but unsatisfying relationship with a man.

Orphaned by the age of four, ANNE FINCH, COUNTESS OF WINCHILSEA (1661–1720) became a royal maid of honour, in which service she met ANNE KILLIGREW. After the flight of James II, Finch and her supportive husband settled in Kent, where she wrote poetry and plays (little of which was published in her lifetime) while battling with depression. Her literary friends included Jonathan Swift and ELIZABETH SINGER ROWE.

Written for Anne Tufton, daughter of the poet's great friend Lady Thanet, 'The White Mouses Petition', in the same tradition as John Donne's 'The Flea', expresses envy of a tiny animal for the physical intimacy it enjoys with the beloved woman.

DOROTHY WORDSWORTH (1771–1855) was born in Cumberland and had a conventional upbringing until she was reunited in her twenties with her beloved poet brother William. In between tours of the Continent, they lived in Grasmere in the Lake District with no servants, spending their days writing and walking. Dorothy was very much the devoted carer, seeing to William's domestic and literary needs, until premature senility made her dependent on him and his wife. Of her own poetry, diaries and letters almost nothing was published in her lifetime.

Dorothy Wordsworth's earliest and dearest friend was Jane Pollard, who married and had eleven children. 'Irregular Verses' was written for one of Jane's daughters, Julia Marshall, but not considered good enough to send.

PERMISSIONS

'Friendship' from *The Scrapbook of Katherine Mansfield* by Katherine Mansfield. Copyright © 1939 by Alfred A. Knopf Inc. and renewed 1967 by Mrs Mary Middleton Murray. Reprinted by permission of the publisher.

'Coming to you' from 'Touch to My Tongue' by Daphne Marlatt in *Two Women in a Bath* by Daphne Marlatt and Betsy Warland (Guernica Editions, 1994). Reprinted by permission of Daphne Marlatt and Guernica Editions.

'On the Road to the Sea' and 'Rooms' from *Collected Poems and Prose* by Charlotte Mew, ed. and with an introduction by Val Warner (Carcanet in association with Virago, 1981). Reprinted by permission of Carcanet Press Ltd.

'Evening on Lesbos' by Edna St Vincent Millay. From *Collected Poems*, HarperCollins. Copyright © 1928, 1955 by Edna St Vincent Millay and Norma Millay Ellis. All rights reserved. Reprinted by permission of Elizabeth Barnett, literary executor.

'Well, then let slip the masks' by Suniti Namjoshi and Gillian Hanscombe from *Flesh and Paper* (Jezebel Tapes and Books, UK, 1986). Reprinted by permission.

'For Willyce' from *Movement in Black* by Pat Parker. Reprinted by permission of Firebrand Books, Ithaca, New York. Copyright © 1978 by Pat Parker.

'If You Came' and 'Old, Childless, Husbandless' from *Collected Poems* by Ruth Pitter (Enitharmon, 1996). Reprinted by permission of the Estate of Ruth Pitter.

'Bury and Dig' from *We Say We Love Each Other* by Minnie Bruce Pratt. Reprinted by permission of Firebrand Books, Ithaca, New York. Copyright © 1985 by Minnie Bruce Pratt.

Poem XVII of 'Twenty-One Love Poems', from *The Dream of a Common Language: Poems 1974–1977* by Adrienne Rich. Copyright © 1978 by W. W. Norton & Company, Inc. Reprinted by permission of the author and W. W. Norton & Company, Inc.

'No Obligation' from *Collected Poems* by Vita Sackville-West. Copyright © the Estate of Vita Sackville-West, reproduced by permission of Curtis Brown, London.

'If I can let you go as trees let go', No. 2 of *The Autumn Sonnets* in

INDEX OF POETS

INDEX OF TITLES AND FIRST LINES

208   *Index of Titles and First Lines*

.

Between Men ~ Between Women is a forum for current lesbian and gay scholarship in the humanities and social sciences. The series includes both books that rest within specific traditional disciplines and are substantially about gay men, bisexuals, or lesbians and books that are interdisciplinary in ways that reveal new insights into gay, bisexual, or lesbian experience, transform traditional disciplinary methods in consequence of the perspectives that experience provides, or begin to establish lesbian and gay studies as a freestanding inquiry. Established to contribute to an increased understanding of lesbians, bisexuals, and gay men, the series also aims to provide through that understanding a wider comprehension of culture in general.

BETWEEN MEN ~ BETWEEN WOMEN
Lesbian and Gay Studies

Lillian Faderman and Larry Gross, Editors

Don Paulson with Roger Simpson, *An Evening in the Garden of Allah: A Gay Cabaret in Seattle*

Judith Roof, *Come As You Are: Sexuality and Narrative*

Judith Roof, *A Lure of Knowledge: Lesbian Sexuality and Theory*

Claudia Schoppmann, *Days of Masquerade: Life Stories of Lesbians During the Third Reich*

Alan Sinfield, *The Wilde Century: Effeminacy, Oscar Wilde, and the Queer Moment*

Jane McIntosh Snyder, *Lesbian Desire in the Lyrics of Sappho*

Chris Straayer, *Deviant Eyes, Deviant Bodies: Sexual Re-Orientations in Film and Video*

Dwayne C. Turner, *Risky Sex: Gay Men and HIV Prevention*

Thomas Waugh, *Hard to Imagine: Gay Male Eroticism in Photography and Film from Their Beginnings to Stonewall*

Kath Weston, *Families We Choose: Lesbians, Gays, Kinship*

Kath Weston, *Render Me, Gender Me: Lesbians Talk Sex, Class, Color, Nation, Studmuffins . . .*

Carter Wilson, *Hidden in the Blood: A Personal Investigation of AIDS in the Yucatán*